Oedipus Revisited

Other Titles by Shere Hite

The Hite Report on Female Sexuality
The Hite Report on Men and Male Sexuality
Women and Love: A Cultural Revolution in Progress
The Divine Comedy of Ariadne and Jupiter
Women as Revolutionary Agents of Change: The Hite Report and Beyond
The Hite Report on the Family: Growing Up Under Patriarchy
The Hite Report on Shere Hite
Sex and Business
The Shere Hite Reader
The Hite Report on Women Loving Women

Shere Hite

Oedipus Revisited

*Sexual Behaviour
in the Human Male Today*

ARCADIA BOOKS

Arcadia Books Ltd
15-16 Nassau Street
London W1W 7AB

www.arcadiabooks.co.uk

First published in the United Kingdom 2005
This B format edition printed September 2007
Copyright © Shere Hite 2005

A catalogue record for this book is available from the British Library.

ISBN 978-1-905147-31-1

Typeset in Bembo by the Basement Press, London
Printed in Finland by WS Bookwell

Arcadia Books distributors are as follows:

in the UK and elsewhere in Europe:
Turnaround Publishers Services
Unit 3, Olympia Trading Estate
Coburg Road
London N22 6TZ

in the USA and Canada:
Independent Publishers Group
814 N. Franklin Street
Chicago, IL 60610

in Australia:
Tower Books
PO Box 213
Brookvale, NSW 2100

in New Zealand:
Addenda
Box 78224
Grey Lynn
Auckland

in South Africa:
Quartet Sales and Marketing
PO Box 1218
Northcliffe
Johannesburg 2115

Arcadia Books is the *Sunday Times* Small Publisher of the Year

Contents

Preface

The Penis and Globalization: Who Are Men Today?

Dear Reader,

Do you like me receive countless junk emails asking you to buy one product or another 'to enlarge your penis' and 'make her happy'?

We can laugh and make a joke and forget it (usually), but here I want to consider how this relates to our current dilemmas, both in international politics and in couples – or may relate. And indicate how we can go forward.

The appearance of Viagra and similar drugs plus the fear of HIV in recent years has increased rather than decreased the focus on erection and 'having a big one'.

Are these just signs of the times, or does erection symbolize the whole system? If it does, the crossroads for us represented by all this is deciding whether democracy/our system can really go on being symbolized by 'a big one', or whether the era in which 'making her happy with a big one' is about to end. Certainly we see a reaction against the 'big one' philosophy: Is the current global war being won by those who act hard, or by 'softies' who negotiate? In the case of Ireland and the UK government, this is one of the burning questions of our times.

Should 'a real man' or government stand firm (equivalent to 'having a big one'), or should 'a real man' search for understanding – in international negotiations as well as private negotiations inside one's family or with a loved one?

Today, personally, many men are in a sexual quandary, finding they can't win no matter what they do: first, they find that putting on a condom can be a problem (while putting on a condom, one can lose one's erection or sexual desire); secondly, they can find that female orgasm does not happen no matter what they do, even with a condom and 'a big one'; thirdly, many men find they are expected now to provide clitoral stimulation to female orgasm by hand (though 'a real man shouldn't have to!'), and so feel extremely confused and blocked -- not to mention feeling a deeper frustration at not being able to think about their own sexual desires and whether this sexual scenario allows them to truly think clearly about their own bodies' desires. Meanwhile some men lose their erections, which they liked having and have been told is the key to success in sex. Some men cut short foreplay because they are afraid they may lose erection while waiting. (The solution is not to think of it as 'waiting', of course.)

The question is must 'a real man' be hard and erect – do we believe this? This a rigid, mechanical way to define men, surely. Men are not robots, after all. Saying they must be 'hard' and 'strong' makes them more likely to be non-verbal, emotionally uncommunicative.

In terms of sex, men could reach higher peaks of feeling and arousal if they did not feel anxious about how they should behave sexually, according to my research with over 7,000 men[1]. During sex as we know it, most men do not allow themselves to explore the full range of feelings they have, especially not with a female partner, since the prescriptions for how a 'real man' should perform during sex are so rigid – therefore most try to follow as perfectly as possible the reproductive scenario as depicted, for example in pornography. Our sexual acts (both female and male) have been channeled into too limited a form of expression; sex could be more interesting if it was not always focused on one scenario, i.e., foreplay followed by penetration, the high point being 'fucking', coitus or 'the act'. Gay men have a different type of sexuality, but often it is also focused on 'a big one' or penetration and a wider range of expression is blocked by the 'real man' ideology, according to my data.

If this 'be a real man – be hard!' sexual prescription also represents the political view that some governments take (those who vote for such political leaders may themselves be victims of the same email ideas …), then the question is, can we repair the political system by redesigning our personal view of sexuality? Or must change come from the top down, i.e., must politicians change, must ideology change, then we will stop getting those pesky junk emails advertising 'get a big one'? In my view, change could work from either direction: we can change the personal (our private lives) and this will change the larger picture (including how men treat women they are dating) or politicians could pass laws prohibiting the taunting of boys, letting kids choose which last name to pick (at age 18 or so), and other measures.

Here let's talk more about the personal sexual side of things for men, though this book includes essays on different sides of men today.

Today many men seem to be withdrawing from sex and performance pressures, even from relating to women. Their stated reasons take many forms, including 1) medical (claiming erectile dysfunction, etc.), 2) looking for 'religious purity' (thus avoiding sex), and 3) deferring 'commitment' ('I need to be free, I need my space') -- or even 4) preferring non-standard 'kinky' sex – and 5) there are other ways. These may be reactions to the cliche pressures (in the emails, for example) that push society's view of men onto men, some men reacting vigorously to resist categorization. If men are informed that they are cheap (via the 'big one' idea seen in pornography, for example), their bodies supposedly mechanically obedient to lurid stimuli (akin to the responses of Pavlov's dogs to a dinner bell), then of course many sensitive men will react by withdrawing.

It would be better to change our outdated stereotypes of sex, give men and women more space to express themselves, than to hang onto traditional ideas of 'the big one' and 'how to get it'. The new male sexuality now developing is part of a larger change many men are quietly searching for, though they have not used these words. (Think of discussions of whether men are spending enough quality time at home, whether men are 'good fathers' . . .)

One of the biggest problems is that a man who has done everything 'to get a big one' and 'not reach orgasm too soon' ('premature ejaculation') can still feel he has not performed well because the woman doesn't reach clearly identifiable orgasm – but in fact, most women don't reach orgasm via intercourse (thrusting in the vagina), despite hype or lip service to this 'what she wants' idea, as seen on TV sit-coms and comedy programmes. While many women enjoy intercourse and identify with and enjoy the man's orgasm, more women regularly reach orgasm via separate exterior stimulation, but this has not yet been integrated into 'normal sex' by most. What a pity that more people do not trust their own experience, rather than culturally-provided information.

How do men feel about the violence to women shown in much pornography? Is it exciting? Do women see erection as a symbol offering them pleasure, or demanding something? Some feel that the erect penis offers not orgasm/pleasure but demands on them, while others see it as a symbol of violence (since in their experience men have combined sex with violence). Many men feel aroused by violent pornography, as do some women – but both are perplexed, asking themselves 'why does it excite me?', and questioning whether 'I am psychologically messed up – am I?' Pornography frequently denigrates women, showing them beaten, black and blue, supposedly liking it (for the money/camera?); at the same time it also denigrates men, cheapening and brutalizing men's sensibilities, blocking their possibility of personal sexual discovery (both of themselves and of others), while re-implanting clichés such as 'a real man is the one with the biggest, hardest erection', and so on. 'It's what she wants. The traditional sexual scenario portraying male ejaculation into the vagina (reproductive act) as the high point implies that men come out as the victors in this combat, since they have orgasm and finish, return to normal, while women still have feelings and want more . . . This is a contorted and unrealistic view of what is really going on, and the potential that can go on.

Such attitudes – young men especially think they should adopt them to be 'real men' – often block men's power to express themselves with women and perhaps with other men. In my ongoing research as described in this book, I find that concepts of sexual arousal and violence can be mixed together during boys' childhoods, especially adolescence, when they are simultaneously pressured to 'be a man' (stop 'hanging out with girls') and 'get a big one'. Both social messages put stress on boys, pressuring them to join the male bonding group -- and cause a traffic jam in their brains that often turns against women, the supposed object of their erection, so that they simultaneously (as young adults) despise and desire young women. This violent cocktail in some boys' minds is tragically informing the spiral of sexual murders and attacks on young girls in the UK and Europe during recent years, not to mention the increase in domestic violence.

In other words, according to my work presented in this book[2], at a time in their development when boys are vulnerable emotionally (pressured by remarks like 'don't be a sissy', 'don't let your mother tell you what to do'), they are also experiencing great changes in their bodies -- they can reach orgasm with ejaculation, their sexual desires become stronger. The negative association that boys begin to have with girls and girlish things is woven into the tapestry of their new sexual identity -- but it doesn't have to be! We can delete the negative consequences of making boys fear women (at the same time that they are supposed to desire them) by stopping the remarks that say 'be a man', i.e., 'don't be a wimp – don't let your mother tell you what to do'. This is a form of bullying that leads to sexual stereotypes that cause lifelong problems between women and men.

Of course violence to women may be discreetly included in the traditional sexual scenario, it is not limited to overt depictions in pornography or to bondage and discipline routines. Thus the erect penis may not be a positive symbol for all women, rather perceived as a threat. But such messages need not be entwined; here we are trying to analyze the various parts in order to see why sexual violence is erotic, and perhaps evolve an even more sexy kind of relations.

In fact men's nature is not what we are often taught: that 'men are beasts whose underlying true natures make them likely to be violent to women' and aggressive in combat; the idea that men 'only want one thing' is incorrect, misleading and dangerous – more or less the same justification used to make 'men of steel, victorious at war'.

It is not surprising that the vast majority of men find it confusing when they actually fall in love, and try to mix body and soul. Traditional sexual messages to men contain outdated ideas dressed up in today's styles that bisect men psychologically, implying that sex is separate from the soul (relatively impure). This bissection makes many men feel subliminally uncomfortable in relationships with women (often expressed as a 'desire for space', 'lack of communication', or 'not enough time at home'), though many are unconscious of the origin of their discomfort. A man in love is usually a man psychologically in a state of confusion and self-searching, since traditional views may seem to inform men (and women) that they are two people -- the sexual animal and the thinking, spiritual individual (one who relates to the 'higher chakras').

Both Western and Eastern traditions (their two religions growing out of the same root, as discussed in the text here) pose a problem for men; both seem to agree that sex is biological (only), thus 'the woman question' need not be a central focus – 'how we reproduce and in what cultural context is our own business'. But is it? Men's sexuality is the reflection of a broader political identity: Taliban extremists in Afghanistan have proclaimed in public statements that they want to 'create a more pure society', meaning one that would be less sexual, a society in which women's bodies are covered, hidden from sight (thus labelling the female by clothing, marking her). Catholic, Buddhist and Islamic priests have declared that only men can be heads of their religions; in the Catholic church, holy men/priests must not have sex; women are seen as 'the devil', sex with a woman as 'temptation of the flesh'. That is an extremely negative conception to give men of women, yet it is part of the traditional cultural backdrop of sex between a man and woman, so that a man may think of sex as a necessary evil focused on reproductive acts, rather than a positive expression of himself in communication with another. (In future, I will publish my theoretical views on the origin of this idea.)

What is men's 'nature'? Perhaps the old sexual scenario with its an ideological view of how men should behave, acts as a brainwashing device for men in general; perhaps men's true personality, if left undisturbed by cultural messages such as 'be a man', would be quite different and less aggressive. Internet junk emails repeatedly advertising 'get a big one!' are going around the world and have a lot of influence, representing Western modernity and today's trendiness -- most people in the West consider these ads harmless but annoying rather than indicators of a cry for help ('I want to be free!'). However these ads present negative versions of who men are, most implying that men have no choice but to be like that (otherwise, the only choice is to become celibate), young men are very vulnerable to these glamorous images, believing that this is how they should be. In most of these ads, women serve the basic purpose of legitimizing male sexual expression as shown – as well as being put into the 'helper' category ('get-me-the-right-breakfast-cereal') or position in the family.

We tend not to take either junk emails or pornography seriously, and believe that they don't represent either our beliefs or the social system – not connecting these statements about sex with what we are doing internationally – so we laugh and joke and think ourselves sophisticated, dismissing these emails as 'silly nonsense about naked people'. Yes they are, but we could use these 'silly images' to think a bit and redesign our sexuality to be more interesting/erotic, and more in tune with global reality. In fact, these 'silly images' tell us something important about our system. We don't have to give up being excited and aroused in the process - this is not about being politically correct. Nor is it about 'the right of women now to be on top' nor 'dominatrixes' nor the excesses of supposed female sexuality seen in some media depictions of 'the new sex'. It is about something new.

Although sex has been seen as trivial, it is a basic social institution with enormous implications for our psyches and political landscape. It offers us an excellent opportunity and means of creating social change: if we sort through our basic thoughts about what sex is, we can contribute to a more positive view of 'who a man is', 'who a woman is', and what our world is.

I would like to hear from you. Please write me or answer the questionnaire in the back of this book.

Shere Hite Ph.D.
17 September 2005
hite2000@hotmail.com

Chapter One

Oedipus In Love: Puberty And The Male Psychosexual Identity

Painful Initiation Rites: 'He's a Mama's Boy!'

As children, most boys feel especially close to their mothers, often preferring to spend time with them than their fathers. However, according to my research, around puberty most boys feel terribly confused as they are pressured by the culture to make a choice, i.e., told they must reject her: 'Don't hang on to your mother's apron strings', 'Don't be a sissy', 'Get out of the kitchen and hang out with the boys, don't tag along with your sister' and so on. Boys are expected to demonstrate their new 'tough identity' by ridiculing and distancing themselves from their mothers, especially in front of male friends, fathers and brothers.

The implications of this have gone unanalyzed in favour of the belief that the change in behaviour boys exhibit around the age of puberty is caused by hormones. The pain of the taunting is laughed off: 'Oh, boys will be boys! Their hormones make them rambunctious at that age.' When, however, many, many moving and sad stories emerged in my research, I began to realize their importance. These are cultural initiation rites, as 'primitive' (or more so) as any tribe in 'darkest Africa'. These initiation rites change the course of men's lives and society. The society has created these rites because of its need to shape men's behaviour in a certain direction, facilitating the social system.

As one of the boys put it: 'When the guys come over, and my mother tries to tell me what television show I can watch, it's humiliating. "Turn that off!" she shouts from the other room, when she hears us listening to it or heavy metal rock videos. I am so embarrassed. I yell back "Shut up!" and turn it up even

1

louder. Then the guys are really impressed – "I guess your mother can't tell *you* what to do!," the biggest one said to me, smiling. I felt accepted then, but it also upset me. I felt like a terrible son and feared my mother would hate me.'

Boys are taunted mercilessly by other boys at school with phrases like 'mamma's boy' if they won't go along with the other boys, or 'stop being a sissy', 'act like a man and stop being a turkey, ape-shit.' They learn that they have to make a choice: in order to enter the male world – to be respected by other males, find a place in the world, get a job – they have to put aside what is called 'feminine', 'gushy', 'childish' behaviour and 'grow up', 'act male', which means to be the opposite of 'feminine'. They often prove this by, in effect, rejecting their mother (or sister) in favour of a group of boys or men, siding with them, talking back to her and so on.

When Boys Leave the Mother at Puberty

Boys are, in effect, expected by the culture to change their allegiance – and identity – at puberty. While as children, many boys feel especially close to their mother, at puberty they must decisively reject her (often in front of witnesses). This 'breaking up' with the mother puts boys under severe mental and emotional stress for an average of about a year, according to my research. Most feel guilty: they simultaneously perceive themselves as being disloyal to a person they love and who loves them but that they have little choice: 'She shouldn't have told me to turn off the music. I didn't want to hurt her feelings by disobeying her and saying something mean to her, but what choice did I have? She brought it on herself.' Others, in a familiar reversal of psychological logic, come to feel that she deserted them: 'You can't trust a woman' and so on.

In other words, boys' psychology is affected at an early age by a traumatic psychological and emotional change in the landscape which is not taken seriously by society – or which is claimed by many Freudian and post-Freudian psychologists to be 'hormonal' and 'natural': i.e., boys' closeness to their mothers 'naturally' ends because male hormones at puberty make boys become distant, disassociated from their mothers, stop feeling close to them. In fact, according to boys' testimony in my research, it is rather the taunts of their peers at school (and fathers), who ridicule them for associating with 'females' and being 'soft' 'like a girl', which makes their behaviour change. Boys in my research also feel disappointed when they learn that their mother's power can't help them very much in the grown-up world: 'I came home crying after school one day and told my mother that a bigger boy hit me. I was stunned when she didn't even sympathize or help me, she just said: "You'd better go back out and hit him even harder, don't come crying home to me. You're a big boy now."' Boys learn that their mothers cannot shield them from making peace with the world of men; they learn that they have no choice but to 'leave' her.

This 'desertion' of the mother leaves significant emotional scars on most boys. Many, feeling guilty about having 'betrayed' their mother, find that this guilt shadows their relationships with other women later as adults. They may feel irritated by what they perceive as a woman's unspoken 'demands': in other words, their own buried memory of their mothers' hurt and pain. Or a woman's love brings up buried feelings of guilt and fear (which may easily become displaced from the mother onto the 'evil' woman who is 'provoking' or 'seducing' them), thus opening the way for a repeated enactment of the 'love must end in rupture' scenario so that they obsessively look for signs of why they should leave the woman.

Many women, as adults, are left to puzzle over men's erratic behaviour during love affairs or marriages, as they observe men waxing first passionate, loving and desirous, then cold and blocking, even hostile and aggressive or violent.

Men have extremely complex feelings of acceptance and denial when they are in love with a woman. In my research, I discovered that most men do not feel comfortable being in love; in fact, most men do not marry the women they most passionately love. Not only did I find that most men say they did not marry the women they most passionately loved but that most men are also proud of it. Most are proud they kept 'control of their feelings'. The reasons for this go back to the love scenario they learned when they were small with the first important woman in their lives: it can't last, it's wrong to stay too close to her, you have to learn to be cold.

Interestingly, in homes where there are not two parents, when boys grow up with only their mothers, they are much less likely to experience the most intense types of this emotional trauma of separation and much more likely to develop stable and equal emotional relationships with women later in life.

Perhaps this psychological dynamic is present in men in other cultures: that is, in patriarchal cultures that drive a wedge between men and women. Arab writer Fatima Mernissi, in *Beyond the Veil*, notes a similar phenomenon in men in Islamic culture, saying that they feel great love for a woman would interfere with their love for and duty to Allah, who, in this context, one could identify as symbolic of other men and the 'male system'.

How Does This Affect Their Sexual Development?

Not only is this confusion of emotions applied to many men's way of seeing women but also to their sexual feelings. Sexually, most boys' early sex lives are subliminally yet potently associated with feelings for the mother. She is the woman with whom they are most intimate. She is the one who knows their secrets, has fed and clothed them and physically touched and held them. Yet at puberty, all this changes.

Boys' puberty, that is, 'sexual awakening', occurs between the age of ten and twelve, when changes in boys' bodies make full orgasm possible for the first time. Most boys begin a very heavy masturbation sex life – mostly in secret, although half of boys share masturbation and perhaps other sexual acts with other boys.[1] 'I remember it as a time of secrets,' one boy relates, 'a whole and complete second world was opening up around me.' Another remembers lying in bed in his room, masturbating while listening to his mother in the kitchen making dinner.

What has not been noted in traditional psychological theory is that, at the same time that sexual feelings are becoming so strong for boys, boys also go through the moral and emotional crisis described above in their relationship with their mother.

Disassociating themselves from their mothers at the same age as they are also experiencing the beginning of strong sexual feelings causes a peculiar love-hate type of sexuality and eroticism to develop in boys in relation to women: a sexuality connected with emotions of guilt and anger.

Because their sexuality is awakening at just the time they are learning to reject and ridicule the mother and 'women's ways' – and because, at the same time, many mothers keep coming back and giving more love and understanding the more hostile and difficult the boy becomes in an attempt to continue the closeness, the pattern is reinforced. Many men come to believe 'women love pain', women are 'masochists'.

In the boys' evolving thinking, the mother's continuing to be nurturing is seen as the mother humiliating herself, which affects how they will learn to define love coming from a woman. William is typical in saying: 'It made me begin to wonder, how far can I go before she will stop being so nice to me? I told my friend the other day when he was over, and we broke some glasses in the kitchen. "Let's don't pick them up and see what she does." We made a bet: I said she would pick them up, and he said, "No, she'll make you do it." I won.'

4

Unfortunately, this all becomes an erotic-love package that some men take with them throughout their lives.

After this, is it any surprise that it can seem normal and erotic for men to want to humiliate women at the same time that they want to kiss them? Is this love? Yes and no. Men are in a bind; most do not see patriarchy as a chain, a fence around them, but instead, believe it gives them 'rights' and 'privileges'.

Although society calls some of the attitudes in men examined here 'human nature', my theory – if correct – is good news because it means that these attitudes are not 'nature' nor dictated by hormones. It means these attitudes are part of an ideology that society puts in place in boys, especially at puberty, through pressure to express contempt for their mothers and 'things feminine' at the same time that they begin to be sexual toward women. These two messages fuse, and the resultant behaviour becomes so commonplace that we call it 'human nature'.

Is there a crisis in many men today – in the male soul and psyche – of which the recent widespread call for a 'return to traditionalism' is only a symptom? Such a crisis will not be solved by the preservation of traditional family values, since to protect the family as we know it does not mean to keep the world safe for loving values, despite how it may sound. Rather it means maintaining the traditional family hierarchy – which insists boys switch their allegiance at puberty from their mother to their father. Why is it necessary to have a family or social structure in which there is a need to choose? The 'traditional family' means (and has always meant): women in the home and subservient, men 'in power' but impoverished and alienated emotionally. To follow the traditional path will lead to further weakening of the social fabric as men, feeling unhappy and cut off, become aggressive, and women, feeling frustrated with trying to make love work, grow cold.

Many individuals are now breaking through the old clichés, social imperatives and stereotypes about the family, trying to build new families of new types and designs, forge real love alliances with people they care for. This can be the wave of the future.

Why Some Men Connect Eroticism With Giving Pain to Women

Sex is danger, violence is sexy – so we are told. Lurid stories of sexual violence scream at us every day from newspapers, films and videos, TV, magazines, the lives of friends, even our own lives. Statistics suggest high rates of sexual violence towards women. During the wars in Bosnia, Serbia, Rwanda and

Sierra Leone, rape was used as a common tool of war. Sadism towards women is a leitmotif of pornography.

But where does it come from, the male ambivalence towards women, the impulse towards sexual humiliation or violence? In my research for *The Hite Report on Male Sexuality*, most men said, surprisingly, that they do not marry the women they most passionately love and that they are proud of this fact. They believe they did the right thing by 'choosing rationally', remaining 'in control of their feelings', even when they lamented their tragic 'lost love'. This, the most profound and important finding of that seven-year research study, seems to indicate that many men feel 'true love' is doomed from the start, that it cannot last. Women do not generally share such cynical feelings about love; they believe problems can be worked out. Why don't men? Where did they learn their point of view?

Through my research on love, sexuality and children growing up in the family, I have developed a picture of men's psychosexual identity and its development that differs radically from established theory.

Earlier research tells us that boys reach puberty between the ages of ten and twelve, when the changes in their bodies make orgasm with ejaculation possible for the first time, and most boys begin a very active masturbatory sex life. What has not been previously noted in psychological theory is that, while sexual feelings are becoming strong for boys, they also go through a moral crisis – a dark night of the soul – regarding their emotional identity and especially their relationship with their mothers.

Most boys' early sex lives are subliminally yet potently associated with feelings for their mothers. They love their mothers; their mother is the woman with whom they are most intimate. They have been kissed by her, have seen her body, felt her arms around them, know her personal habits in the bath, watched her combing her hair – and they know sex is part of her life or part of the hidden things they cannot know about her life. 'My father started explaining about sex,' one boy relates, 'and my mother told me about menstruation, how girls sometimes bled between their legs. I began using pornographic pictures and magazines…'

Breaking Up With the Mother: Must Love Always End?

'Breaking up' with the mother puts boys under severe mental and emotional stress. In many, it creates a lifelong pattern of believing that love cannot last, cannot be counted on. Most boys feel guilty for adopting these new behaviours; they simultaneously feel they are being disloyal to a person they love and who loves them, and that they have little choice but to do so. Others, in a familiar reversal of psychological logic, come to feel that their mothers deserted them. And thus they take up the idea that 'women are not to be trusted'. Others take with them a lifelong belief that strong, passionate feelings cause terrible suffering and are to be avoided.

In other words, at the same time that boys experience a sudden flowering of sexual feelings, they are hit by a traumatic change in their psychological and emotional landscape: they go through a period of emotional turmoil which culminates in the 'desertion' of the mother. This crisis can affect their relationships with every other woman in later years: they may feel irritated by what they perceive as women's unspoken 'demands' – which are their own buried memories of their mothers' hurt and pain. This can make it hard for them to love and accept love, because a woman's love brings up feelings of guilt and fear that are displaced onto the 'evil' woman who is 'provoking' and 'seducing' them.

This confusion carries over into many men's sexual feelings. At puberty, many learn to mix up sex and violence. Dissociating themselves from their mothers while simultaneously experiencing the beginnings of strong sexual feelings causes a peculiar love-hate response to develop in many boys in relation to women: a sexuality connected to guilt and angst. Many learn to associate eroticism with hurting women. And when mothers, even as they are being rejected and ridiculed, keep coming back and offering more 'love' and 'understanding', the more hostile and difficult the boy becomes, so the pattern is reinforced. The mother's continuing nurturing is seen as a form of self-humiliation that affects how the boy will learn to define the 'love' that comes from a woman.

Too many boys construct a sexuality towards women that combines desire and contempt. To show desire is to show contempt; it's all part of the same thing during sex. This is how it was with their mothers; they must love and want them, while at the same time distancing and disrespecting them.

Thus men's physical and emotional relationships with women contain elements of love and hate, desire and repulsion. It can seem normal and erotic for men to want to humiliate women at the same time that they want to kiss them.

A man's sexual identity can be so dangerously distorted that, loving and hating the mother (and by extension, all women), he can feel perfectly justified, when sexually challenged, in striking out, engaging in emotional resistance, exploding in psychological or physical attack. It 'feels right' sexually to combine intense desire, even love, with pain and aggression, domination and humiliation.

This is not to say that it is politically incorrect to have sex that includes ideas of power – how could we avoid them, growing up in the culture we do? But at least we should know what it is we are doing and why: not stupidly call it 'hormones' and glorify it, claiming we have no choice but to live as we do.

It is not inevitable 'male nature' to be ambivalent or even hostile during relationships with women. Obviously not all men are. These attitudes are part of an ideology which society endlessly reiterates to boys, especially at puberty. Pressure on boys to express disdain and contempt for their mothers, at the same time that there is pressure to begin to be 'sexual' toward women – these two messages become fused together forever causing a block in boys' minds. This block becomes so completely built into structures in the mind that we can't 'see' it anymore.

Clearly, men do fall in love with women; still, they usually continue to put 'masculinity' before love, often hiding their true feelings outside the home environment. It is more important to them to be 'one of the boys' than to work out a relationship with a woman, no matter how wonderful it makes them feel.

There is a crisis today in masculinity, of which the recent widespread 'return to traditionalism' is only a symptom. The dilemma cannot be solved by appealing to traditional family values since, as we have seen, that is where the syndrome is perpetuated, women considered 'lesser', and men emotionally impoverished, distant. The only solution to the Oedipal dilemma is a change in the male codes, in men's value system – that is, masculinity as currently structured. Since this way of thinking has led to the problematic desire in men to 'conquer all' (for example, to win wars, conquer the environment, be on top of love and relationships, politics and corporations) this would have a positive effect internationally.

A new kind of male heroism is required, a reinvention of the male psyche, a fresh identity for contemporary culture.

Do Men Really Enjoy Their Definition of Sexuality?

Does sex really reflect who men are? Let's expand the boundaries; isn't male sexuality more than the simple cliché of 'getting hard and thrusting'? The definition of sex as we know it puts men into a rigid harness of 'performing reproductively' rather than expressing themselves and the many things they may feel. Although it seems so obvious, do we know what 'male sexuality' really is? After all, it is impossible for us to know exactly how much of what we see men do is 'natural', 'male sexuality' and how much is learned or reinforced behaviour.

The current definition of male sexuality in terms of a driving desire for 'penetration' is clearly culturally exaggerated. Male sexuality comprises a much larger, more varied group of physical feelings than those ascribed to it, having been narrowly channelled by the prevailing culture.

Surprisingly, when looked at more closely, the definition of sexuality put forth by the current social system is actually quite negative. Although it is often thought that men are very 'pro-sex,' while women are 'anti-sex', in fact, most women think in terms of a much broader concept of sexuality than the reproductive model we have come to believe is 'natural'. The basic cultural ideology refers to sex as a body function, an instinctual 'animal feeling' that is the opposite of a spiritual feeling. In this value system, 'animal feeling' is somehow not respectable, even 'dirty', something 'without soul' (animals in early Christian tradition did not have souls), 'brute bestial behaviour'. How do men feel about this idea of their bodies? While sex need not be always 'sweet', never 'dirty and passionate', the idea of sexuality as completely cut off from feeling – sex as something 'subhuman' that animals (who reputedly have no feelings) do and therefore not part of our humanity – is a strange definition, and not the most erotic idea either. This idea of 'sex' alienates people during sex and robs them of their full experience; perhaps it does the most damage to men, since they learn to think that women are from another planet, women 'don't need to have orgasm the way men do' or something to that effect.[1]

In my study of over 7,000 men of all ages and backgrounds, I learned that men's sexual feelings represent a much broader canvas than that which they generally use during the reproductive ritual with women commonly called 'sex'. Most men complain of feeling restricted to worrying about 'performance' during sex. Many men say they would like to reinvent male sexuality: they feel on a gut level that somehow they are missing out, that no matter how much sex they have, they are still unsatisfied on some level. This accounts for the frequent belief that it is 'men's nature' to change partners often.

Current definitions of sex put enormous pressure on men to have frequent sex and to think and see both women in particular and the world in general in mostly compartmentalized sexual terms. In fact, the 'male' ideology and the lifecycle it creates often rob men of the chance to enjoy love, by warning them against 'confusing' a passionate attraction with 'love', warning them against real closeness, warning them 'you can't trust women,' 'don't let your sex drive confuse you, it's lust you feel, not love' and so on, stating that a 'real man' should be 'independent,' remain 'free' and unmarried for as long as possible, avoid being 'tied down'. Real men should seek to have sex with as many women as possible. Real men don't fall head over heels in love. The result of all this training of men to control their feelings is that many men become alienated from their deeper feelings and are no longer sure what they do feel.

Our culture's lessons to men have been so strong that few men are able to get past them, to create their own personal sexuality or transcend such double-standard messages that alienate men from themselves and from those they are attracted to. But a new sexuality is possible. This is by no means to downgrade men's traditional 'lust' but to redefine it. As one man puts it: 'Passion is one of the most beautiful parts of all sensuality: the desire to "possess, to take, to ravish and be ravished, to penetrate and be penetrated". But is physical love real love? While love is caring, love is also passion and desire, the desire to belong to, to mingle with, be inside of another. Part of love is a sheer physical feeling a desire not only to have orgasm and "sex", but to lie close while sleeping together, to press chests together, so tightly, as tightly as possible; to lie feeling the other breathe as they sleep, their breath grazing your cheek and mingling with your own breath; to smell their body, know the smell and taste of their genitals, to feel with your finger inside them. To let them feel inside you too. What is love? Love is talking and understanding and counting on and being counted on, but love is also passion and the deepest intermingling of bodies. In a way, body memory of a loved one is stronger and lasts longer than all the other memories.'[2]

[1] For further information on sexual behaviour in early puberty see, Alfred C. Kinsey (with Wardell B. Pomeroy and Clyde E. Martin), *Sexual Behaviour in the Human Male*, Sanders, Philadelphia, 1948; Shere Hite, *The Hite Report on Male Sexuality*, 1981 and *The Hite Report on the Family*, 1994.

[2] For more information on male attitudes towards the female orgasm, see Shere Hite, *The Hite Report on Female Sexuality*, 1976.

Chapter Two

Boys And Their Fathers: Distance And Longing

Boys in my research for both *The Hite Report on Male Sexuality* and *The Hite Report on the Family* state over and over, in the most poignant and moving statements, that they did not know their fathers very well, that their fathers rarely talked to them about their feelings, personal thoughts or relationships. In fact, most boys said that they had never had a real conversation with their fathers about a personal topic. Most expressed a longing to have had some deeper experience of communication and acceptance.

Boys often become fascinated by the power of this emotionally silent and mysterious monolith, the 'older man':

'I didn't know my father, really, I didn't know what went on in his head. He went to work, he came home, he got angry at odd moments and everybody seemed to have to help rearrange things so his anger would go away and he, the god, would be pacified. I used to ask my mother what was I supposed to be like – him?

'I always identified with the son in *Death of a Salesman*. I didn't want to be that salesman either. So I tried to go along outwardly with the behaviours they all expected of men, damn it, say as little as possible to avoid conflict (or discovery that I was not all I was supposed to be, cracked up to be, I wasn't a "typical man"). Funny thing, one day my one-year-old son said to his mother (when they thought I wasn't around): "Why doesn't Daddy say anything?" I had managed to look just like my dad looked to me.

'I felt a sharp pain inside me, almost a stabbing blow. I went and sat down on the sofa and hid my face in my arm, I was crying. It also hurt me when my wife, after my son said that, just murmured something like, "Oh, your father's just like that. He's in his own world, he can't help it" – as if she were alienated too. There was just no place to turn. It was then I knew I had to change. I had to make a different life for myself and everyone around me.'

Like the Michelangelo's depiction in the Sistine Chapel of Adam reaching for God's hand in *The Creation*, in which their fingers never quite touch, men often feel that tantalizing sense of 'almost, almost'. They can almost touch their father and yet there is a distance that is unbridgeable. They are left with a feeling that he is unattainable, 'other' and that this is how it must be.

This incomplete relationship affects many men forever. They attempt to reach the father, try to make him recognize and see them, the son, at work. This is the same fight that women can have with men in love relationships, essentially trying to get men to 'open up, be more communicative, relate fully', to see them. A cycle persists of the younger man, or a woman, not being able to 'get through' to the grown-up, perfectly closed man, consequently feeling less and less loved, coming up against his silence and distance.

My research shows, secondly, that the harsh initiation rites of puberty make boys learn to bond with and/or fear men in groups; they learn to try (at least outwardly) to conform to the behaviour of the men in groups around them forever after.

These boyhood events, which hitherto have neither been noticed nor taken seriously by Freud or others, came out strikingly in my research, showing that boys at puberty learn a bitter lesson; they speak repeatedly of their extended pain and emotional turmoil during a period of one to two years around ages ten to twelve. What they reveal is that most of them felt very close to their mothers early in life, liked to be with her, felt comfortable at home with her, however, around ages ten to twelve, extreme pressure was put on them (usually by older boys at school) to 'shape up', 'be a man', 'don't stay home with your mother', 'don't let your mother tell you what to do'. If they don't heed these messages, they will lose status within the group and possibly even be beaten up or kicked out.

Most boys were emotionally distressed during this period: they didn't want to betray their mother by taking on new, disdainful attitudes, but eventually they came to realize that they have no choice but to join the male group and become 'one of the guys'. To many, this feels like diving off a high diving board into a deep pool, not knowing how to swim. This trauma is created by society – and need not be. However, it is usually attributed to hormones and not questioned. While debate in the UK has decried the bullying of boys by other boys in school, no laws prohibit this kind of psychological bullying.

Later, many boys as adult males apply the same logic at work, concluding that they must conform to the group of men in an office or a corporation (or on a construction site), or they will not fit in – and certainly not get ahead. For example, at work, many men – having internalized these lessons about staying with the boys and avoiding the girls to ensure acceptance as 'part of the men's group', feel nervous with the new presence of career women, and about breaking rules of conformity to male groups around them.

Although joining the 'world of the fathers' is a frightening experience for many boys and men (and women) – as boys describe feeling alone and insecure, suddenly in a new, colder and more competitive world: one that they say over and over that their fathers did not explain to them – conquering it can become the biggest adventure they undertake in life. Later, however, according to my research, sometimes on becoming such a 'fearsome, male monolith-power person' themselves, men feel very unsatisfied and disillusioned.

Many younger men now want to find a new way forward. Often men today, as much as women, want to change the atmosphere inside the workspace, but it is difficult for men to behave differently at work than outside traditional notions of male-bonding behaviour. As boys learned, the approval of other men ('the older boys at school') is very hard to come by, and once you've got it, you'd better not lose it (especially not by behaving with disloyalty: i.e., hanging out with women) or you'll be ousted from the group. Not 'playing the game' with the guys could cost them their job.

Corporate executives today could feel unconsciously uncomfortable being 'disloyal' to the men's group at work by working closely with women on an equal level with them or promoting women above men. If men can break the spell of this fear they learned so early in life, a fear that to many has become unrecognisable, 'forgotten', then the meritocracy that was promised can finally become a reality.

In other words, siding with 'a girl' against a group of men, promoting a woman into a completely male office, can be considered an act of treason, so many men today feel torn between their ethical sense of what is right, and their desire not to 'rock the boat'. Once the realization is clear that the situation inside corporate boardrooms resembles the pubertal boys' bully system at school, and that it doesn't have to – that it is counterproductive to today's workspace – things can feel freer and change quickly.

Various factors have come together to set men thinking, embarking on a momentous interior transformation that has as yet to go public. Most no longer want the extreme 'revolution' of the 1960s but they also don't want the 'return to traditional manhood' of the 1980s; they want a new third way, something they are inventing.

This change in perspective has been in the making for some time. Related to history not hormones, an entire century of social experimentation underlies many men's deep desire for change. They may have lived through twenty-five years of rethinking, or some were raised by mothers and fathers who had also done major re-thinking. Although today's media speaks more often of the changes women have made, men have changed dramatically too. During the second half of the twentieth century, men revolted en masse against the family: first, the *Playboy* revolution (symbolized by James Bond films, showing the ever-single, glamorously non-monogamous Agent 007), followed by 1960s flower power, civil rights and Black Pride, as well as the birth control pill and the 'sexual revolution'. With all these movements, men stressed they wanted more individual self-determination, less conformity (although in some cases they wrongly targeted women as the cause of their feeling 'tied down'). Through the feminist movement of the 1970s, men's thinking about their identity was challenged in a new way. All of this created a heady mix of ideas in the minds of many men who by the 1980s were ready to call a halt and 'go back to traditional values'. But could they go back? The divorce rate passed 50 percent, and the number of people living as 'singles' neared half. The 1990s saw a media focus on extreme versions of sex – sadomasochism, Internet pornography and sexual violence as fun: 'you're not a real man unless you like it – and participate'.

Out of all this twentieth-century turmoil, what emerged? While media images of men stressed the importance of being 'different', there was simultaneously great pressure on men at work to conform and 'be traditional' – give off an image of respectable, traditional stability, if one wanted to get ahead.

Still today, many men find they are coping by living with split personalities: one for work and another for 'outside' or 'private time'.

Although we have one of the greatest opportunities in history (after all, how often do we get the chance to design a new society?), will men be able to overcome their fear (all but lost to conscious memory) of other men, their irrational bonding with a system that claims to help them, prefer them – as if they could not create another, new and better system?

14

Quite a few men in my research say they have problems with male authority figures, speaking of feeling torn between wanting to be 'a New Man' and wanting to work with the 'male establishment authority figures', the daddies and patriarchs of fable – so exalted in mythology, novels and elsewhere, their archetypes are all around us (and that their own distant relationships with their fathers early in life helped convince them exist). During the 1960s, it was fashionable to declare that 'you can't trust anyone over thirty'. 'Young men' believed that old men were all corrupt, had made some kind of trade-off with 'the system', so that they were no longer honest or relevant.

How does a 'young man' make the transition to being an 'older man' in authority without making too many compromises to still be true to himself, stand for something – and like himself? This can be done, but it is not easy. In today's context, the question of women's status especially challenges men's integrity and sense of fair play. Men at work have very ambivalent feelings about how to treat women in the new situation; obviously, 'letting women be equal at work' is an idea with justice on its side – but should they go ahead and work easily with women, blend in, make new choices – or should they try to please the older male authority figures who may prefer signals of an old male-bonding variety? The challenge is for an individual man to understand well enough both sides of his identity, his new thinking and his older training, so that he can elegantly move the entire situation to another stage: make the new world of work valid for everyone concerned – the women there, his boss and also himself.

Men today, according to my research and the statistics around us, seem to say that they are quietly undergoing a revolution on their own terms, in their own inner values and beliefs – beliefs about the importance of work, how work should be structured, how private life should be lived, how time should be spent. Many men are rethinking the ultimate values of life, what it means to be alive and part of this world.

Today's men have begun to question more than ever their own place in the sun: if work is not exclusively theirs, then what is? Does it matter? How much time should one spend at work, how much in private life? Is time at work 'quality time', real life? Today's sons, who often grew up with parents of the sixties and seventies, claim that the world they will make will be radically different from the world of 'the fathers'. Will this be true? What will the sons of Women's Liberation make of the corporate world?

Fathers and Sons: Will the 'New Man' Change Corporate Culture?

Originally, corporations did not pose a challenge to the traditional social order because 'men were hunters', whether in a natural jungle or the corporate one. However, with the arrival of large numbers of women in the workplace, the office no longer resembles the traditional social order. For several decades, corporations did not challenge men's traditional identity. Except for secretaries, it was mostly men who inhabited the corporate landscape, so nothing was out of sync with the 'traditional social order': male competition could follow the Biblical models of Cain and Abel, sons versus fathers (or sons obeying fathers), brother versus brother or brother working with brother, male groups pro or contra other male groups. Traditionally, corporations have been kingdoms in which 'sons' and 'fathers' by turn competed with each other or worked together: younger and older men jousted or fought together for power, glory and money.

One way of understanding relationships between men at work is the Freudian view which, claiming biological infallibility and therefore to be eternally and universally true, sees men in combat (competition) in which the son fights his father for power: i.e., Oedipus kills his father to 'gain his mother'. But while Freud might claim it is 'basic male nature' for sons to try to overtake and dominate their fathers, one does not find this scenario portrayed in classics such as Shakespeare's *Romeo and Juliet* (the son of Montague is not angry with his father for making his life difficult, nor does he try to wrest power from his father), nor does Arthur Miller portray the eldest son of Willie Loman in *Death of a Salesman* as trying to dominate his father; the son simply wants to leave home and get away from the whole family. On the other hand, many men in corporations do feel that 'the fun of it all' is competing with the other guys; younger men sometimes do dethrone older men, taking their crowns.

The view that human nature is unchangeable would imply that men can't change, that sons will always 'by nature' challenge fathers. Is this true? Aren't other interpretations or explanations possible?

My research has turned up two quite different reasons for male attitudes to each other, whether fighting or bonding, inside corporations. Both imply that flexibility is a big part of human nature, and that change is not only possible but likely: that what we call 'human nature' is very much shaped and created by society. First, men's loyalty to other men (and desire to be accepted by them, work with them) is, ironically, increased by the lack of closeness most boys felt growing up with their fathers. In the great majority of cases, the relationship between father and son is not close, although there are exceptions. Boys learn their understanding of relationships with men from this early relationship, no matter how distant it may have been. If it was distant, they learn that relationships between men are distant. They tend to repeat this model with their own sons.

The Pressure to Play with Boys, Not Girls

As one man in my research remarked: 'I was called a sissy by a PE teacher when I didn't want to play football with boys who were older and heavier than I – then when I did participate, I was kicked in the face and called sissy when I cried. I was humiliated and angry.' Another said: 'I was told, "Be a man, not a sissy!" during sports by my father. It hurt because I always wanted to please my dad. My lack of competitive spirit left me open to these charges. I felt like a traitor.'

Team sport is supposedly especially 'manly': playing with the group is better than 'proving yourself' as an individual: 'In 10th grade, when I was injured in football and had to sit out most of the season, I realized that I liked not playing better than playing. But I didn't have the internal strength to quit sports teams, even though I grew to like running alone more.'

Sports are a hotbed of pressures to 'be a man', according to most boys. As one boy puts it: 'I was an intellectual kid who always had his nose in a book, but I was driven into even more isolation by demands to be a jock and good at sports. I couldn't handle them at the time. In high school I used to get beaten up quite often for having no interest in sport or fighting, and for being a "closet fag". In essence, I was ostracized by my peers during much of my high-school education.'

Boys also describe a lot of pressure not to associate with girls ('You're a sissy if you play with girls'), not to have girls as friends ('Girls are for sex') and to spend their time with other boys. As one man remembers: 'I was always being criticized for playing with girls, but I felt that playing with girls was just as much fun as playing with boys. My attitude bothered my parents.'

Another said: 'At about eleven my father criticized me for wanting to play with the next-door neighbour, who was younger than me, because she was a girl. Another time he blew up at me for spending the afternoon at a girl's house rather than doing something like being out playing football.'

17

And one boy, who liked to cook with his mother, was told by his uncle that: 'Boys like to do things with their mothers, but as they get older, they find that men are the ones they want to do things with. Why don't you try getting involved with some of the other boys who have hobbies, like fixing up their cars?'

With pressures like these, it is no wonder that men so often feel uncomfortable and uneasy, after they 'grow up', when they fall in love with a woman – no matter how happy they may be with her. In fact, most men in my research say that they feel uncomfortable being in love: one described it as 'a dis-ease'.

If boys are told repeatedly that they are wrong to hang out with women, how can a man suddenly change when he is an adult to 'find it natural'? This boyhood scenario – that we as a society could change by forbidding the practice of bullying and taunting boys with such epithets – is leading to many unhappy marriages and relationships in which the man works seven days a week, tries not to 'hang out at home', comes home very late at night after a long workday 'with the boys'. It is clear now why so many men feel happier, more like they are 'doing the right thing', when they are 'out at work with other men' than 'at home', even though they say they are happier at home.

Does the system of work and male privilege truly benefit men? Does it reward them for trying so hard to be 'manly' – or does it deprive them?

Father, Behold Thy Son

Sons crave their fathers' approval but often find an emotional chasm between them. Participating in sports is one of the few ways fathers and sons spend time together: bonding together against an opposing 'team' (or animal being hunted) is the only way in which most men are allowed to achieve emotional contact with their father in the traditional 'family system'. Being on a team, men are allowed to feel excitement together (but not directly towards each other); sharing emotions in a 'team' makes emotional sharing 'legitimate', since the emotions are directed (ostensibly) at something other than each other. Thus, the men have an emotional interchange, an emotional climax, sanctioned by the society because it is channelled through an abstract 'third party'.

Watching team sports together is part of boys' socialization process, especially at puberty and after. Through seeing 'the game', men learn about 'what men do' in groups. The appropriate etiquette to use with other men is crucially important for men in their business and work lives, as well as in their social relationships with other men. Which emotions and facial expressions should they show? The players show little emotion (except for outbursts of anger); 'staying in control' while still 'showing power' are the watchwords. Through sports viewing, men can vicariously enjoy the feeling of being part of a group of men.

In this way, 'male psychology' is learned through sports. Being able to form a team with other men is an essential element of the male genderizing process, learning the proper way of behaving to fit into the world of men. Boys learn quite early that there is no masculinity: one cannot be truly 'male' without joining and conforming to a male group – unless one is a heroic loner, a rebel. Examples of this 'alternative role' are Shane, the hero of the 1953 Western movie of the same name, actor Marlon Brando, most male rock stars and even Jesus. Yet this role does not truly offer an alternative or much diversity in terms of room for other personalities, since the 'rebel' is in fact almost the mirror image of the father: he is simply challenging the father for power, setting up a different power centre. The symbolism of the son's struggle with the father is always central to this psychological planet; all ethical battles take place within this inner circle, with this cast of characters.

The father (or the heavenly archetype of the Father) is the only one the son must 'fear'. This leads to an alienated relationship: boys describe enormous distance in their relationships with their father but also a feeling of longing, wanting to reach the father or somehow communicate emotionally with him.

In this psychological landscape, relationships with women are in another sphere and do not have the same rules. Oddly, however, most men in my research say they look to women when they need someone to talk to and for emotional support; most married men say it is their wives who are their best friends, although women do not say the same about their husbands.

This background of distance from the father, combined with pressure to 'be with men', puts men in an odd, uncomfortable position – that sometimes takes unusual forms, as this man describes: 'During adolescence I had erotic fantasies of being caressed and approved of by my father. I was well into my twenties before I began to work on these feelings. What I realized was that I had very powerful urges of wanting love and confirmation to flow between us. It makes sense to me, now, that I wanted some reinforcement for puberty's confusions.'

Some men today believe that these definitions of masculinity as distance hurt not only women (when men grow up and can't talk to them) but also themselves, and they are now engaged in an inner debate about their tradition and power. They no longer believe that male dominance is a matter of biological inevitability or superiority, but a historical circumstance that should be changed. On the other hand, the movement to 'return to traditional values' seeks to ignore any such self-questioning, even labelling men who think this way as 'wimps'! Maintaining the traditional family hierarchy – women in the home and men 'in power' – is, however, a futile attempt to turn the clock back.

This does not mean that the 'New Man' should be 'soft and cuddly' or that the 'New Woman' must show her 'true sexy animal nature' in order to be 'progressive'. It means that the way forward is to create a new blend of traditional and current values, a more solid type of sexual morality and pleasure for the future, one including equality. Stop bashing boys.

Boys and Their Fathers

The tragedy of the father-son relationship is explained by one man: 'I used to go hunting with my dad during my boyhood. Unfortunately, I have always been a very poor marksman (my hands shake too much). I gave up hunting after an incident in which my dad and I were duck hunting in a boat with some other men. I had just brought down a duck, and we paddled the boat over to pick it up. As we reached it, I was astonished and delighted to find it still alive and looking well. It seemed so cute and attractive I envisioned taking it home with me, nursing it back to health and keeping it for a pet. One of the men picked it up and proceeded to beat its brains out over the side of the boat.

'All the time I was growing up, it was funny – I was closer to my mother than my father, she was the one who was more loving – but I knew it was my father's opinion of me that counted, it was his approval that I really wanted. Why? I don't know. But I'm still that way, in a sense: I love my wife, very much, and we are happy together – but to be really happy, I want more than anything to be part of the world of men and to be recognized by other men as a man and successful.'

In a very real sense, relationships between men matter to men in a patriarchal society – even more so than male-female relations. Men look to other men for approval, acceptance, validation and respect. Men see other men as the arbiters of what is real, the guardians of wisdom, the holders and wielders of power.

But are men able to be close to each other in our society? What do men learn from their fathers about being men? Paradoxically, even though men regard one another as important, most are afraid of becoming too close. 'Feelings' for other men are supposed to be expressed only casually and should not go beyond admiration and respect. Thus, men's relationships with one another tend to be based on an acceptance of mutually understood roles and positions, a belonging to the group rather than an intimate personal discussion of the details of their individual lives and feelings. As one man put it: 'We are comrades more than friends.' Our culture simultaneously glorifies and severely limits men's relationships, even relationships between fathers and sons. Still, men often feel a deep sense of affinity and comradeship with other men.

When asked 'Are you or were you close to your father? When you were a child, were you affectionate?' almost none of the men replied that they had been or were close to their fathers:

'He was always busy. He was a quiet man of few words, though extremely witty, and articulate – and very loving and affectionate, which slowly disappeared as I got older to eventually become a formal, stiff, cold relationship.'

'Not particularly. We played sports, talked politics. I can talk to him about non-personal subjects, but we are not personally close.'

Most men were not able to talk to their fathers:

'He is a very quiet and simple man, I guess the fact that he is quiet never allowed me to talk to him as much as I would have liked. As a child we were pretty close because he did things with me that I enjoyed, like baseball, football, etc. We would pass time together rather than talk.'

'I've never said anything important to my father.'

Even physical relationships with their fathers as very young children seemed to have been off-limits to many men; when asked whether they had been physically close to their fathers as children, very few could remember being carried or cuddled by their fathers – although they often remembered being spanked or punished.

Some men wanted more affection: 'During my childhood, my relationships with my parents were unpredictable and insecure. I always felt that my father wanted me continually to prove my feelings and loyalty, but I felt that I couldn't rely on my parents to come through for me. I think that I learned early that boys don't show affection, and hence stopped being affectionate with my mother also at an early age. Now I see physical affection as a sign of assurance, trust, etc. – the opposite of unreliability. But I feel uncomfortable with it, I'm afraid to reach out and give it – I think it looks inappropriate, too feminine, silly. Maybe this is why I don't connect sex with feelings much – it seems too nerve-wracking and I don't feel comfortable with it.'

These were some of the saddest stories in my research: the poignant tone of missing something, longing for something – a deeply lonely feeling – emerged in man after man. Surprisingly most said that there had been no father-son talks; that they had learned only from example and disapproval or condemnation and ridicule when they did something 'wrong'. As one puts it: 'We didn't do much together, he said I played baseball like a girl.'

Most boys did not spend a lot of time doing things with their fathers: 'I discovered the male role more from watching James Cagney, Humphrey Bogart and James Bond than from my father. At least, a male as I would like to be.' And another: 'We did not really attend sports events together or play much except to kick a soccer ball around occasionally. Because of the nature of his business, we were not able to spend much time together except when we were on vacation… I don't remember much about those trips.'

Thus, the testing grounds for masculine identity, according to men in this study, are:

1. Most men said there had been great pressure on them as boys to be interested in and participate in sports, and compete with other boys in physical strength – competitive type sports.

2. There was also pressure to have 'made it' sexually – penetrated a girl!

3. On the other hand, there was pressure not to play with or associate with girls, not to have girls as 'friends'.

4. Hunting was another testing ground of 'masculinity' or toughness.

5. Fraternities and clubs also often involved initiation ceremonies designed to test 'manhood' – to see if the applicant could withstand humiliation or 'teasing'.

As men describe their childhoods, they often speak of the distress they felt trying to learn the stressful male role, which demands complete obedience, strength (or the appearance of it), a competitive attitude, success and control. Mothers are usually blamed for 'bringing their sons up like that', but in my research men describe feeling or having felt these pressures coming from the older men around them (older boys at school, their fathers and older brothers, uncles and so on, as well as from television, cinema and other media). Most described their father as demanding these characteristics and behaviours, although most also described their fathers as very distant, (often due to the father being caught in his own attempt to comply with the stereotypical male role in which the father is always stable, never showing 'weakness' – i.e., feelings – or 'burdening' his family with his worries). As one man puts it: 'My father told me: work hard, never complain and don't spend all your time with your mother. If I cried, he was humiliated and told me to be a man – or to go to my room and stay there until I got control of myself. Other than that, I hardly knew him.'

Another probably articulated what many men had missed and longed for when he said: 'I think a relationship between a father and son is one of the most, if not *the* most, important in society today. Yet it is probably the most troubled. A father-son relationship must not be fraught with hatred and a tense tyrant-subject relationship; this will ultimately destroy one or the other or both. It must be a wide open relationship in which the man will give of himself so that his son will become the man he wants to become.'

Gender Conformity: How Boys Learn They Have to 'Be Like Other Guys'

One of the easily visible lessons boys learn about how to be male is to stay in control – especially of emotions, but also of information, of friendliness, not to be too effusive, to keep a cynical eye peeled for others' motives, to look out for number one. A man should look, act and behave like other men – but be on top. The unspoken subtext that boys are learning via these messages about behaviour is gender conformity.

Most men say they do cover over feelings, especially those of pain or frustration – or even great happiness or enthusiasm – lest they be teased, in an effort to be 'one of the guys':

'I was raised to conceal my actual emotions and to display whatever emotion I believed was most appropriate, to maintain or achieve control of a social situation. Now I hope I can kick the habit, even though other men may laugh at me.'

'Men are trained at an early age to disregard any and every emotion and be strong. You take someone like that and then wonder why they don't and can't express feelings. Not only that, they are supposed to be a cross between John Wayne, the Chase Manhattan Bank and Hugh Hefner. We are only human, for Christ's sake.'

Strangely (or perhaps not so strangely) most men never quite feel they live up to all the rules: the majority of men, when asked their opinion on any topic, will soon respond: 'But don't ask me, I'm not really typical, so my opinion may not be valuable or valid.' Although on one level most men accept traditional definitions of masculinity, on another they doubt whether they can ever completely 'measure up'.

Underneath the outward conformity necessary for personal survival (in most cases), there often lurks a man who feels he is not really quite 'what a man should be'.

Teaching men to deny their feelings has roots in Biblical tradition: the ultimate lesson to men to deny their own individual desires and feelings and to follow laws, rules and orders unflinchingly is the story of Abraham on the mountain preparing to kill (sacrifice) his own son in order to follow the will of God the Father. The same story also exists in Islam. No more wrenching story of a man learning to kill his own feelings can be found.

Some men, when asked how they would define masculinity, expressed a kind of rebellion against the rules: 'They say masculinity is someone who thinks he is superior to the opposite sex. That masculinity is easily defined by muscle, or masculinity is someone who never cries, is always tough. Let's face it, I'm so full of the "masculinity" crap, it is sickening. I consider myself one-quarter masculine, one-quarter feminine (oh, if those jocks could hear me now) and one half fighting for something in between. I cry when I feel like it, yet there is pressure to not cry ("Young men don't cry"), but then I tell myself, the hell with everyone else, I feel sad and crying is the only way. The other part of me says: "Boy, you are a real sissy crying, you are showing a weak character." The other part (feminine) says, "Whoever claimed that if a man cries, he is weak? It takes a stronger person (man) to cry, you know." That's the kind of thing I'm fighting. The answers, I am trying to find them.'

Learning to be 'tough' and stay in control of emotions puts men in a difficult situation when trying to express love or negotiate a relationship with a woman, the whole 'male' role value system is antithetical to the role a person needs for a warm and generous, emotive and empathetic relationship – a relationship in which the number one rule is: don't try to dominate the other person. Men would usually not try to do this in a friendship with another man, but as 'a man' not 'dominating' a woman could seem 'unmanly.' And therein lies the rub – the dilemma for a man in love with a woman.

Chapter Three

The Uncelebrated Beauty And Diversity Of Male Sexuality

The Sexual Pleasures of Being Male

What is a man's 'sexual nature'? Most men have been taught to think of their bodies as sexual tools in the harness of reproductive activity. The canon goes like this: 'You must get an erection, you must insert it into the vagina, and you must have an orgasm – but not too soon!' Starting in the James Bond 1960s, a man was thought odd if he did not want sex with a woman of reproductive age, preferably young, at the drop of a hat: a 'real man' should always have a hard penis, 'have it ready', gun loaded. There is an assumption that 'men are sexual beasts with raging hormones': in other words, that we are all 'natural creatures' underneath society's 'veneer' and our sexual nature is biologically structured. Male sexuality is in particular is understood in terms of its being of a 'bestial nature'.

According to this popular hypothesis, a 'man is a beast who can't help himself…certain things turn him on and he gets going and just can't stop, it's nature's way of making him deposit his seed here, there and everywhere…' In recent years, have men become less focused on erection of the penis or 'drive for coitus' *à la* James Bond? Have they reconnected their sexuality and their emotions, or are most men still basically worried about how big their erection is?

Our culture's lessons to men have been so strong that few men are able to get past them to create their own personal sexuality. We live in a culture that has taught us that sex is reproductive activity; that other activities (such as masturbation or oral sex with no coitus) are less valuable, even evil. In this scenario, men are focused on achieving erection – although many women make it clear that an erection is not the key to their sexual satisfaction.

27

The fashionable drug Viagra, the 'miracle pill' that offers men an erection 'on demand', reinforces the idea that erection is the be-all and end-all of male sexuality – the only way a man can be sexual – and also reinforces the belief that erection is mechanical, more related to bodily deficiencies than to a relationship or emotions. In fact, if a man does not have an erection, there may very well be a problem in his relationship or his situation, not in his penis. However, although emotions and erection are clearly connected, many men would rather believe almost anything else: 'Well, I guess when you get middle-aged, this is bound to happen.'

This seems to mean that the penis is simply connected to a more or less self-generating set of hormones or body mechanisms that should operate, no matter what a man is (or is not) experiencing. People have often made fun of the 'toys for boys' erector set idea of masculinity – wooden blocks boys put together to form buildings, atoms, etc. – joking about whether men would also use a wooden kit to build 'the erection' too? Others insist skyscrapers and pointed objects are 'obviously' representations of the penis...

Such remarks give boys the impression, when they are growing up, that they have a foreign object between their legs – that the flesh on their body called 'the penis' is not a part of their overall being, not their 'self', but just a 'rude piece of meat' located 'down there'. The epithet 'he thinks with his penis' is further damaging since it implies that when men have erections and desire sexual connection, they are not thinking but being 'stupid' or 'animalistic'. 'He's a jerk' is an epithet derived from 'jerk-off', meaning someone who masturbates or 'plays with himself'.

The truth is that the penis is a delicate part of the male being: one that responds with exquisite sensitivity to every nuance of emotion a man can feel. However, society has tried to insist that 'a real man' should 'get hard' at will, whenever he decides it is 'appropriate'. But it is impossible to will an erection into being. Trying to do this has caused a great deal of psychological pain and self-hate in many men – and often in their partners too, as both took the 'lack' of erection as a sign of the lack of love.

Erections come and go in men, during sex and during sleep. A man who is kissing a loved one may stop, worrying: 'I can't get an erection now, so I'd better not keep on with this.' But in fact, he could continue being physical with his partner. Many men stimulate themselves during sex, masturbate for a minute or two, to make sure their penis is hard at the very moment they want it to be. This approach works perfectly for most men. On the other hand, a man can enjoy 'sex' even without having an erection – although of course erection itself is pleasurable for men and no one wants to deny this. But since orgasm in women is generally not caused by 'penetration' or coitus, no matter how much a woman may enjoy the feelings (but not all women do), therefore there should be no pressure on a man to have an erection 'to please the woman' in most cases. The definition of sex has been focused on the reproductive act, to the detriment of other activities, because we have evolved from a culture that wanted to increase reproduction. Now, however, most of us use birth control.

Our sexual acts have been channelled into too limited a form of expression; sex could be more interesting if it was not always focused on one scenario – 'foreplay' followed by 'penetration' (insertion), the high point being 'fucking' (coitus). Sex should be a varied individual language of ways to touch, caress and excite oneself and another person – whether that means stimulation by hand of both people or sharing the excitement of a sexual fantasy or oral sex.

The fear of HIV has increased rather than decreased the focus on erection; many men only became more nervous faced with putting on a condom and not losing the erection or their sexual desire. Further new pressures added more complications; not only are men asked to use a condom, they are expected to provide clitoral stimulation to orgasm in many cases and to be emotionally sensitive to their partner, not turning over and falling asleep immediately after their own orgasm, for example. While some men breeze through the art of providing clitoral stimulation by hand or mouth to orgasm, others prefer to think the supposed 'G-spot' inside the vagina is the answer to the changes in sexuality that women have been talking about.

Masturbation is the one time when men express their sexuality without a focus on reproduction or coitus and do not worry about erection. As one man puts it: 'I have more or less two sex lives, one with my wife and one with myself.' Many women in my research are shocked to learn that a man who is their regular partner also regularly masturbates: 'Why would he want to do that, when he can have sex with me almost any time he wants?' Men in my research say they enjoy masturbation or having sex alone because they can fantasize about whatever they want and there is no pressure on them to perform for another person. Also, laboratory studies show that self-stimulated orgasms in both men and women are stronger.[1]

Men could enjoy their sexuality more if they would focus less on penetration during sex and more on expressing themselves sexually in whatever form their emotions take, while making space for their partner to do the same. No man should ever fear lack of erection, as he has only to reach down and touch himself...

Men's Great Sensuality – A Potential As Yet Untapped?

Why is male sexuality so closely identified with intercourse? Have men missed the boat because of the total focus society teaches them to have on intercourse, or because of the (also learned) dominating, goal-oriented definition of their sexuality? Even if now clitoral stimulation to orgasm is included before intercourse, as long as 'sex' equals 'foreplay,' followed by 'vaginal penetration' (why not call it 'penile enfolding'?) and ends with male orgasm in the vagina, this means that sex will still be focused on intercourse and retain its overly structured definition. Men will continually be made to worry about 'performance pressures' and 'what a man should do'. Defining sex as basically intercourse holds men back from getting to know and appreciate their own sensuality, forcing them into an unnecessary, anxious preoccupation with erection.

The focus on a man's perceived responsibility to achieve erection and perform coitus, 'to perform his duties as a man', tends to cut off many men's erotic responses before they even get started. For example, many men cut short 'foreplay' and physical affection because they are afraid they may lose their erection – which they have been taught is necessary to enjoy sex and which it would be 'shameful' to lose. But men could reach much higher peaks of feeling and arousal if they did not feel anxious about how they 'should' behave sexually and if they did not focus so much on reaching orgasm.

Men's denial of their great sensuality is significant because it is part of the overall denial by men of their feelings and emotions. As we have already seen, a 'real man', it is said, should learn to always be 'in control' of his emotions. Thus the traditional definition of masculinity tries to close men off from their full capacity to feel joy, sadness and love, experience the world and life. Men have everything to gain from leaving behind the mechanical view of 'male sexuality' and at the same time developing a greater appreciation of their untapped sensuality, their own capacity for enjoyment and expression. Men's experience of their own bodies has been cut off, limited, falsified by the culture's insistence that 'male sexuality' is a simple mechanistic drive for intercourse.

'Sex' could be deconstructed to become something with infinite variety, not always including intercourse or even orgasm (for either person). It can become part of an individual vocabulary of many ways to relate physically – including activities that express anger, tenderness, passion and/or love, depending on the current feelings of the two people – a way of expressing a thousand different feelings, saying a thousand different things.

Can men imagine a new conception of male sexuality and sensuality not necessarily focused on intercourse or orgasm? Would men like to diversify and expand, eroticise their sexuality – become less constantly active, sometimes more passive, more receptive? Have most men ever experienced sex as less orgasm and more passion?

Why is intercourse so important to most men, or why is it portrayed in pornography as being the sole object of most men's lust? The usual assumption is that 'men are made like that by their hormones, they can't help it.' However, this is an assumption, not a fact. On the other hand, it is relatively easy to show – as this research does – that there are many cultural messages to men coercing them to define themselves in this way.

Not only are men encouraged to want intercourse by a culture that says that this is how 'real men' behave, but men are also left little other choice of ways to be truly close and intimate with other human beings. Men are brought up not to be 'sissies', to control their feelings and to be as dominant as possible in every situation. Only in 'sex' are men encouraged to 'let their hair down' and be tender, affectionate, passionate or 'out of control'. Only through sex are men encouraged to relate emotionally to women. If men are cut off from each other – first from their fathers, by the 'rules' of male behaviour and then later, following that example, from their friends, at least in the sense of being able to talk intimately and show affection – then men must turn to women for close companionship. But at the same time, they are 'supposed' to dominate those women. It is in this confused atmosphere that men and women experience sex.

Even more confusing, it is in the moments of sexual intimacy that most men feel most free to talk about their feelings, problems, hopes and dreams. This, in combination with the need we all have for close, warm body contact, can make a sexual connection almost the most important need a man has. And the central focus of that sexual connection is intercourse – only intercourse, perhaps, has the symbolic overtones to make this connection deep enough. But the symbolism has both a positive and negative aspect.

Origins of the Definition of Sex as Intercourse For Men

In fact, the current definition of sex as 'foreplay' followed by intercourse and ending with male orgasm in the vagina as the 'right' way to have sex has not always been the definition of sex. Everything we think of as 'male sexuality' is in very large part a reflection of the values and needs of the society we live in and the culture we have inherited. The definition of sex as we know it was begun approximately 2,500 years ago for the purpose of increasing the population. It was at this time that the Hebrew tribes returned from the Babylonian exile, a small, struggling group. These tribes passed a law, the first such law we know of, saying that henceforth all sexual activities other than heterosexual intercourse would be illegal. The Old Testament constantly warned against other forms of sexuality, including 'spilling one's seed' (masturbation), oral sex, and the sexual practices of the 'heathens' (surrounding tribes), especially the Babylonians.

This officially promoted focus on reproductive activities, and the attendant glorification of intercourse, was important for the small tribes, since only through increasing their population could they become more powerful, consolidating their hold on their territory, cultivating and harvesting more crops and maintaining a larger army with which to defend themselves.

This definition of sex also reflected a new male ascendancy in society, in that henceforth the children were to belong (along with women) to the fathers (or husbands), which had not previously been the case. The Hebrew tribes, possibly influenced by traditions of invading Indo-European or Aryan tribes, were organized with a patriarchal social structure – that is, ruled by men: women and children were owned by a husband or father, who in turn owed his allegiance to a male king, who in turn owed his allegiance to a male priesthood and a male god. But the Babylonians, like many other societies of the time, for example the Canaanites, did not worship one male god, or even one god; furthermore, many of the gods they did worship were female, and indeed it was women who were the priests. Queens in these societies were frequently as powerful as kings, if not more so, going back to an early non-patriarchal tradition, which was probably very widespread during an earlier period.

The exact nature of this tradition is still a matter of debate[2], but many scholars now agree that, based on archaeological and written evidence, very early periods had quite a different form of social organization from our own. Some scholars refer to these early societies as 'matriarchies', although very little is known in the popular culture about them; other feminist scholars have objected to the term since it implies that these societies were the simple reverse of 'patriarchy', that is, that women owned the children and ruled men, rather than having a more complex tradition of their own, possibly more egalitarian. However, although there was a great variety of social organizations among these groups, it does seem clear that women were held in higher esteem than men, and that women were usually in general charge of the temples and distribution of food and goods. Whether women also were warriors is not known – although many goddesses were addressed as warriors. But these societies were certainly not male-dominated. Both the physical relations between individuals and the family structure were in all probability quite different in these early forms of social organization than in the later patriarchal structure.

The following is a simplified version of some hypotheses of the changes that seemed to have taken place over a period of a thousand or more years, perhaps sometime around 8,000 to 5,000 BC. The very earliest societies may have venerated women because it was thought that only women could bring forth new life. Some scholars believe that in such societies, dating back earlier than the Babylonians or the Egyptians, the relationship between intercourse and pregnancy was not known, and so the male role in reproduction was also unknown. Additionally, the earliest families we know of did not consist of the mother, father and child, as we know them today, but rather a group that included the mother, sisters, brothers, aunts, uncles and children. Children could be brought up by various members of the group – the biological mother having had the choice of whether to 'stay at home' with the child or not. In other words, there has not always been the close tie between the biological mother and child (nor the father and child) we consider 'natural' today; children of many mothers mixed together and were brought up by many members of the group. In fact, the concept of private property may not yet have existed, or may have been very weak or unimportant to the society; certainly children were not 'owned'.

At present, we do not know the exact dates of the changeover from pre-patriarchy, with its religions deifying both goddesses and gods, but we do know that the struggles went on for many years, even centuries, and in many locations. It has been theorized that when the male contribution to childbearing became known, possibly around 10,000 or more years ago, this knowledge coming at different times to different societies, there began a gradual shift to more male involvement in religious functions, and gradually to the system of patriarchal social order in which men now are almost entirely dominant. Scholars are only slowly piecing together fragments of records to understand what happened in these early times; much remains to be understood. However, some scholars see the Old Testament as, among other things, representing the story of the early patriarchal struggle against goddess worship and female-oriented societies and the transition to a male-dominated, monotheistic society. The history of Greece, together with the chronological changes in Greek mythology, has been seen as representing a changeover in thinking from goddess worship to God's ascendancy.[3] A similar change from the ascendancy of queens to the ascendancy of kings can be seen over several centuries in early Egyptian history. The transition from Cretan culture to later Mycenaean, mainland Greek culture is another example. However, these interpretations, while steadily gaining adherents, are far from orthodox. On the other hand, scholars generally agree on a recent revision of the extent of our fully human ('civilized') history: according to latest estimate, complex human societies existed as far back as 40,000 years ago – quite an increase over what had previously been thought.

What was the role of intercourse in pre-patriarchal or 'matriarchal' societies? Even in early patriarchal or transitional times, intercourse was not thought of romantically or in terms of being the greatest physical pleasure there is, more pleasurable than other forms of intimacy and sexuality, but basically was practised for reproduction. This was true, for example, in most periods of Greek and Roman history. What must sex and physical relations have been like even earlier, then, 20,000 or 40,000 years ago, when it may have been believed (at least for some time) that women became pregnant simply by lying in the moonlight? When intercourse was not an especially noted symbol in the society? Were sexual feelings tied to religious ('fertility') group activities, rather than 'romantic' personal activities? Or were sexual feelings and orgasm linked to 'romantic' personal feelings, while fertility activities (whatever they may have been) were linked to group or religious activities? There is some evidence that the latter may have been the case, but we honestly do not know what people did.[4]

But to return to the present, it must now be clear how completely sex, as we know it, is tied to our own history and social organization. This definition has come down to us from the early Judeo-Christian laws, which became, in fact, the civil code of the entire West, whose laws are still basically those of our present civil code.[5] In addition, old church laws are still enforced by many churches today. For example, the Catholic Church says that women should not use birth control, since the purpose of sex is reproduction, and since women should make their bodies available to their husbands for this purpose at all times, and further, that the fathers will own the children. It is also important to note that other societies, like those of Japan, China, India and the Arab world, also defined sex in much the same way once they became patriarchal: that is, physical relations regulated for maximum reproduction, with the children being owned by the father, is the rule. In other words, the reproductive definition of sexuality is an inherent part of a patriarchal society: in order for men to control a society, it has been essential for men to control reproduction and to own the children.[6]

Sexuality today is changing – probably largely due to the fundamental changes brought about by the industrial revolution. Increasing population is not as necessary to the power of a society as it once was, since we now have very large populations and even more importantly, machines can now do much of the work large populations once performed, from farming to defending a country. Therefore, as society feels it no longer needs to encourage reproduction to the extent that it once did, birth control is becoming more and more acceptable, and male ownership of children (and marriage) less crucial, with 'living together' arrangements more accepted.

However, this change has not yet deeply affected our idea of what sex is or could be. Even though we frequently use birth control, we still generally follow the traditional reproductive definition of physical relations, centred on intercourse. But, as seen in this book, some men are beginning to question the assumptions of our culture about 'male sexuality' and our definition of sex; even though the issues are just beginning to surface, there is a gut feeling on the part of most men that something is wrong – that although there are beautiful elements to sex as we know it, somehow there are unnecessary problems, too.

Deconstructing Intercourse: Is It the Greatest Male Sexual Pleasure?

How much of men's desire for intercourse is due to our culture's insistence that all men should seek and want intercourse, that it is 'natural' for men, and how much is due to an individual man's desire to have intercourse with a particular woman for his own personal reasons? We can never know exactly.

But it does seem clear that, without the accompanying cultural symbolism and pressures, intercourse would become a matter of choice during sexual activities, not the *sine qua non* or dénouement toward which all sexual activities move, as it now is. This is not to say, of course, that men and women will not continue to enjoy intercourse with each other when they want, but simply that sex could be more enjoyable for both people if intercourse were not a 'requirement' – if intercourse were a choice and not a given. Sex does not always have to include intercourse, and sex would become much freer if intercourse were not always its focus.

Intercourse is at once one of the most beautiful and at the same time most oppressive and exploitative acts of our society. It has been symbolic of men's ownership of women for approximately the last 3,000 years. It is the central symbol of patriarchal society; without it, there could be no patriarchy. Intercourse culminating in male orgasm in the vagina is the sublime moment during which the male contribution to reproduction takes place. This is the reason for its glorification. And as such, men must love it; intercourse is a celebration of patriarchal culture.

Surely such a definition of sex is guaranteed to make a man feel that his needs are serious, worthwhile, and important – at least his need for orgasm and his need for stimulation of the penis to reach that orgasm. This fact is so obvious that it is usually overlooked or taken as a given: a simple 'biological' imperative. However, our definition of sex is, to a large extent, culturally, and not biologically, created. Women's need for orgasm and for specific clitoral stimulation to reach it is not honoured or respected in the traditional definition of sex. Certainly it is not enshrined within an institution, as is the male orgasm. Although the institution we know as 'sex' was probably created to lead to male orgasm in the vagina not because of male dominance but only because of the society's desire to increase reproduction, nevertheless, the man himself, as eventual owner of the child and of the woman, must surely feel secure in the knowledge that this ritual honours him and enshrines and venerates his orgasm. Thus men feel that their orgasm during intercourse is good. However, men usually do not attribute creation of the institution to manmade society; they look, rather, to biological or religious sources – in other words, 'it's just the way things are', or as one man put it: 'Intercourse is a heavenly blessing which God created for man.'

In addition, this cultural institution, this symbolic rite, is aided and attended to by another person, a woman. If male orgasm is the sacrament here, the woman functions as the priest. This woman not only gives the man a sense of being accepted and desirable on an individual personal level, but also gives him a further sense of acceptance by joining in and catering to the sequence of events that culminates in his orgasm. This woman, with perhaps varying degrees of enthusiasm, but almost never with withdrawal once 'sex' – the ritual sequence of events and especially intercourse – has begun, helps him along toward his orgasm and a sense of pleasure.

Both men and women feel that this is woman's role. And yet most women still do not feel that they have a similar automatic right to clitoral stimulation to orgasm – and even less do they feel they have the right to touch or stimulate themselves to orgasm – and still less do they feel they have the right to insist that men cater to their needs (especially if the woman is not also catering to the man's needs). Why does our society consider it perfectly acceptable to assume that 'sex' can be defined as intercourse to male orgasm every time with clitoral stimulation to female orgasm included only sometimes or not at all while considering it outrageous to define 'sex' as clitoral stimulation to female orgasm every time, if it almost never or only rarely included penis stimulation and intercourse to male orgasm?

Furthermore, in traditional intercourse, the man was on top of the woman, adding to the symbolic impact of his culturally decreed superiority. The fact that he almost always had an orgasm while she did not further encouraged him to think of himself as superior, more successful, healthier and more sexual (or more fully evolved, as some contemporary psychiatrists have recently asserted), as opposed to the 'weaker' woman who was not able to have a similar climax, despite the fact that she almost certainly was not getting the right stimulation.

In other words, during traditional intercourse, the ancient patriarchal symbolism of the man on top comes to the fore: the man on top, 'taking' his pleasure, the whole force of the social structure behind him, telling him that what he is doing is 'good', 'right', and that he is a 'strong male' – with the woman looking up into his eyes, not resisting and hopefully celebrating these feelings with him, saying 'yes, you are great'.

And there is yet another aspect: the symbolic acceptance of the sperm by the woman. As the woman accepts the semen, she accepts an intimate part of the man and, at least symbolically, accepts the idea of carrying the child for him. Intercourse in patriarchy, as we remember, means power because a man can say: 'I own this woman. I can make her pregnant.' This was equated with power in early patriarchy, because earlier societies had not known the connection between intercourse (sperm) and pregnancy; they thought women reproduced by themselves. After this connection was discovered, the erect penis gradually became the dominant symbol in society that it remains to this day. Before this, the female body – and especially the vulva and breasts, as seen in the thousands of 'fertility goddess statues' that have been unearthed – was the primary symbol.

This is not to say, of course, that intercourse does not feel good to both women and men in its own right. However, superimposed on these basic feelings is an enormous cultural symbolism that has become so ingrained in all our minds, both male and female, that it is hard for us to be sure just why we do like intercourse.

Another implication of this ideology is that intercourse makes a male a man before other men; intercourse is a form of male bonding. Boys are told that they cannot have intercourse: only men can. Thus intercourse becomes a test of status and dominance through which males prove their membership in the male group – not only the first time but over and over. One basic definition of a man is someone who has intercourse with women. Why is this? Would this be a test of 'masculinity' (whatever that may be) in a society that did not hold reproduction as a primary value? Historically speaking, men's identification with intercourse (and the emphasis on 'performance') grew out of a social system that wanted more soldiers and farmers. In fact, for quite a long time, intercourse was not connected with love or romantic love, nor was it even considered necessarily the main thing a man would want to do: Greek men, for example, often seemed quite happy having sex among themselves – considering intercourse with their wives a duty necessary basically only for procreation. No doubt this was the way the wife viewed it as well, since her orgasm was not a consideration. Was she having orgasms through masturbation? Or with her women acquaintances with whom she spent the day? No one knows.

Even earlier, Hebrew men had to be admonished in the Old Testament not to 'spill their seed' – i.e., masturbate – or practice sodomy, but instead to have vaginal intercourse. This implies that they may have found it more pleasurable or convenient to masturbate or to have other sex for orgasm, and that in fact this may have been their custom.

In patrilineal society, then, intercourse for a man has the whole force of a society's approval behind it: he is doing what the entire society says he should be praised for doing, and the woman's acceptance of him functions as a symbol of the acceptance of him by the entire social order – and especially by other men. However, intercourse does not bestow the same feeling of social acceptance upon women; the meaning of intercourse for women is quite different. Although the woman, as agent for the society, fulfilling her socially dictated role as nurturer and helper, is bestowing acceptance and approval (and the stimulation for male orgasm) on the man, she is frequently not getting any of these in return. In addition, society does not praise her for having intercourse. Her orgasm is not enshrined, and she may be looked down on by the man for having 'given herself'. This is another issue, one which was covered in *The Hite Report on Female Sexuality* – but it is well to keep in mind how differently our culture has chosen to reward the two sexes for the same activity.

Still, women do enjoy intercourse; and women and men do often transcend these cultural meanings in their personal lives. Although intercourse has been a symbol of masculinity and male power, it need not continue to be so. As women gain equality – economic, social, and legal – intercourse can lose these exploitative connotations to become once more a simple thing of beauty and freedom and, above all, a choice.

Finally, the point here is not that men are wrong for liking and wanting intercourse, but that they should be freed from feeling that they must have intercourse to have true sex – and to be 'real' men. It would be senseless to 'blame' anyone, either men or women, for traditional and stereotyped attitudes and behaviours which we all learn every day and endlessly hear repeated around us. The point now is to re-examine the part intercourse plays in our lives, to reassess our personal definitions of sex and try to create more individual, and more equal, forms of physical relations.

In fact, it may be, on some level, just this cultural catering to men during intercourse that also makes men feel uncomfortable, uneasy and ambivalent about it. Do they want to feel the object of so much unequal attention? Do men want to feel that the success or failure of the whole ritual rests on their performance? The ideal of masculinity glorifies men at the same time that it would de-humanize them.

Is 'male sexuality' a simple hormonal fact, or does it reflect society? Could it be different?

Male sexuality is central to the definition of masculinity – and masculinity is central to the worldview of the entire culture; in a sense, it is the culture. Therefore, what we are looking at here is far more than male sexuality: it is a way of life, the world itself, a culture in microcosm. To discuss sex is to discuss our most basic views of who we are, what we want life to be and what kind of a society we believe in.

Is there a difference between how individual men feel about their sexuality – and how the culture says they should feel?

Intercourse is said to be one of – if not *the* – basic ingredient of sex for most men. In fact, the overwhelming majority of men studied did not want to have sex that did not culminate in intercourse and male orgasm. Why is what we know as 'male sexuality' so identified with intercourse? Is it for reasons of physical pleasure or are other, more symbolic, cultural forces at work? Intercourse is such a dominant symbol of our society that its actual identity has hardly been studied, and the right questions not asked. The standard interpretation of male sexuality says that intercourse is the greatest pleasure a man can have. And yet, isn't this a bit simplistic?

The mechanistic definition of male sexuality as basically a question of getting an erection, penetrating the woman and reaching orgasm is in large part a reproductive pattern created and perpetuated by our culture – not an inevitable expression of the 'male sex drive'. Men are more complicated than that; male sexuality is just as much tied to emotions as female sexuality is.

Is it possible that men are missing out on a large part of their sexuality, sensuality and enjoyment by so totally equating sex with intercourse?

Is Men's Focus on Coitus 'Natural'?[7]

Why do men want intercourse? Most men like and want intercourse. However, the reasons are surprising. It is almost universally assumed that what men want from intercourse is their orgasm. And yet, in my research, men point out over and over that they can easily have an orgasm from their own stimulation (and often a stronger one than during coitus). In fact, what men want from intercourse is something else: 'I like intercourse more psychologically than physically. I get a lot of physical pleasure from intercourse, but I can also get that from masturbating. The physical feeling of moving my penis back and forth inside my lover is pleasurable, but probably not as intense as a good hand job or fellatio combined with hands. Psychologically, though, there's much to want – the anticipation of putting my penis inside my lover, knowing I'm going to be surrounded by her, warmed by the inside of her. Then when I first slowly enter her, I want the instant to last and last. I like to stop moving, just lie there, and think and feel,

"This is happening to me. This is so neat. I feel so good.""

Boys are brought up to equate intercourse with manhood: 'I felt (and still do, to a lesser extent) incredible pressure on me to prove my manhood by screwing women. This pressure made it harder on me to meet women and have sexual relations with them. I had to do it; if I didn't there was something wrong with me. Also, it was supposedly so great, look what I was missing. This pressure bred its own miserable rationales, e.g. "women always want it, even when they say 'no'." Thus, I had no excuses. If I couldn't find a woman to fuck, it was my fault I was a failure. I feel this pressure helped retard my sexual growth and experience and placed undue importance on fucking.'

The culture has taught men and women that intercourse symbolizes masculinity and male identity; the historical reason for this – the creation of a social system that would maximize reproduction – has long been forgotten, but the symbol continues to be glorified. That is, in a patriarchal society, intercourse (or the erect penis, ready for intercourse) symbolizes masculinity. More specifically, just as the erect penis symbolizes masculinity, intercourse symbolizes the acceptance of the erect penis – i.e., the validation of masculinity by both the individual woman and the entire culture. How much of men's desire for, and identification with, intercourse is due to a culture that tells men that this is what they should want? Some men did not answer whether they liked intercourse, or why, but simply stated that intercourse is what men do – the natural and inevitable expression of 'instinctive' male 'sex drive':

'Sex identifies me to myself as a man; sex admits me to full citizenship in my species and my world. Without sex I would regard myself as somewhat less than a man and somewhat less than a person.'

'I feel that our Creator made men with a penis and women with a vagina for a reason, and that's for intercourse.'

'Being a healthy male, sex is very important to me. The purpose of sex is a normal function of the human mind and body.'

Many men's answers seem to suggest that they are not sure how often they would like to have intercourse, but that they are fairly sure that they should be having it more often than they are, or that other men are having it more than they are. There is also a vague sense of disquiet in some answers in which men say that it is not theirs to choose how often they will have intercourse: that at any moment the woman may 'shut them out' and refuse to have intercourse with them. In fact, the cultural pressure on men to have frequent intercourse is based on a purely mechanical definition of masculinity, in which the desire or 'need' for intercourse is related solely to a man's supposed inner hormonal cycles or some other mysterious 'innate' sexual urges. Of course, how often a man has or wants to have an orgasm is a separate matter from how often he has or wants to have intercourse.

In fact, it is possible that our culture has pushed men to 'want' intercourse more than they, without this pressure, might. Certainly it is possible to have sex without having intercourse. And certainly, men have the right to go without sex entirely or not have sex with a partner, if they want, as almost all men in fact do for certain periods of their lives. Men should not be made to feel that they 'have to' have sexual intercourse to prove they are men or for any other reason.

Erection and Patriarchal Identity (Definitions of Self)

In a culture that says a man is not a man unless he likes or wants intercourse, a man who 'cannot' have intercourse (does not get an erection) will be encouraged to see himself as 'less than a man'. The demeaning term 'impotent' has usually been applied to lack of erection and, of course, means 'lack of power' – that is, a lack of the ability to impregnate a woman, which is the basic 'power' of patriarchy. Many beautiful types of closeness have been given second-class status by a social structure that once wanted and needed to increase reproduction. Even though the idea is now so antiquated that birth control is practiced almost universally, we still insist on describing a man without an erection as 'impotent,' a failure – rather than seeing the whole human being, and the appropriateness of many degrees of physical arousal.

Of course, erection and intercourse are pleasurable to both men and women; however, it is one thing if a man cannot get an erection when he desires one, and another when he feels he must produce one. In fact, a man need not have an erection to give a woman an orgasm, since orgasm in women is usually created by manual or oral stimulation of the clitoral and vulval areas – or at least not by friction of the penis on the inner vaginal walls.[8] The need for erection to 'satisfy a woman' has been greatly overemphasized. And most men fear 'impotence' more because they think they will appear unmanly or a failure, than because of fear of loss of pleasure.

The cultural emphasis on erection, which leads to an ever-present fear of lack of erection, forces most men to become focused on getting and maintaining an erection during sex. This in turn forces the activities to revolve around the erection, influencing the timing and sequence of events. Physical relations could develop a more spontaneous feeling if the importance of erection were greatly de-emphasized. Older men, who may have trouble achieving or maintaining an erection have been ridiculed and made to feel 'less than men' by the society; in fact, often their diversification and rethinking of sexual pleasure has made them 'better' lovers than younger men.

And some men did, in fact, feel repulsed by the cultural vulgarization of their sexuality – for example, in advertising images of how 'a real man is just naturally crazy for sex'. Many men voiced a strong reaction against some of the ideas of the 'sexual revolution', including the idea that men should want and have sex and intercourse at any time or place, not needing an emotional relationship or feelings as the context for sex:

'It's depressing. I don't usually have sex just for lust, it's more spiritual. I'm old-fashioned, romantic. I'm a dreamer, I guess.'

'I hate the sexification of everything in which oppressive sex roles are just more visible and blatant, and everybody goes around acting terribly sexy and fucking each other's brains out, and sex is openly alluded to in aspirin commercials and toothpaste promos, etc. I think that's sometimes called the sexual revolution and I hate it.'

The pressure on men to be 'sexual' and to have frequent sex has been particularly strong during the last twenty years, or perhaps especially since the 1940s and World War II, with the increasing equation of masculinity with aggressive characteristics. In Victorian times, for example, men were often urged (by doctors and others) not to have sex and orgasm too often, lest they drain themselves of their 'vital fluids' and become weak. Today just the opposite is urged. The idea of a male 'biological need' for penetration and intercourse, an aggressive, animalistic 'sex drive' was incorporated into the so-called 'sexual revolution' of the 1960s.

Male 'Sex Drive': Real or Imaginary?

The term 'male sex drive' is part of larger reproductive ideology; yet there is no biological or physical proof of a male 'sex drive' for intercourse. Although both male and female do have a need (or 'drive') for orgasm from time to time, there is no evidence that men biologically 'need' vaginas in which to orgasm, or that there is anything hormonal or 'instinctual' which drives men toward women or vaginas. People tend to believe that 'there must be a sex drive for doing the act, otherwise the species would not exist, reproduction would not be taking place.' This is a very simplistic and naive view of the facts.

Even if something so rudimentary were true, this would not mean that men should be harnessed into a reproductive straitjacket, being told that the be-all and end-all of their sexuality is to 'get hard' and 'penetrate a woman', 'having an orgasm there inside her'. While that is pleasurable for some men some of the time – and some women some of the time – clearly male sexuality is about so much more. Typically men have blamed women for 'inhibiting their sex drive', but in fact, it is the straitjacketing by the culture that is inhibiting men's sexuality.

Many kinds of physical contact are enjoyed by the other mammals just as frequently as – or even more frequently than – coitus, which is practiced only when females are in estrus. Humans do not have estrus in anything like the same way. Most mammals spend more time on grooming and petting each other than they do on specifically sexual genital contact, as many primate researchers have described. Mammals and other animals also masturbate and quite commonly have homosexual relations.

Our culture seems to assume that since sexual feelings are theoretically provided by nature to ensure reproduction, therefore intercourse is – or should be – 'instinctive' behaviour. Yet when one looks at other animals it is obvious that other forms of touching and genital sexuality are just as 'instinctive'. Masturbation may even be a more natural behaviour than intercourse, since chimpanzees brought up in isolation have no idea how to have intercourse, but do masturbate almost from birth. If, as is so frequently asserted, intercourse really is 'instinctive' and all else 'unnatural', why do we need laws and social institutions that both glorify and require intercourse (especially in marriage), while setting up grave penalties and taboos against other forms of sexuality? Men can rethink their sexual assumptions with great advantage to themselves.

44

Is Resistance to Sex and Intercourse Political or Neurotic?

Many men are frustrated and dissatisfied with sex with women, or have mixed feelings about it, even while they say they want more. The reasons for this are not unchangeable: the society has created inequality and separation between the sexes, which originally involved a struggle over the control of reproduction; this now permeates almost every aspect of sexual relations between men and women. These attitudes are slowly beginning to change.

Why aren't some women enthusiastic about sex with men more frequently? First, because women feel exploited sexually: they must help the man have his orgasm but must not effect the stimulation they need for their own. Given our definition of sex, the fact that men usually want sex more often than women should come as no surprise. Sex provides efficiently for male orgasm, and inefficiently and irregularly for female orgasm; sex is defined so that the woman expects to help the man orgasm every time, but the man is not realistically informed about how to help the woman orgasm, and the woman is told it is wrong to stimulate herself. Therefore, should we be surprised that men want sex more often than women do? Sex as we know it is a male-defined activity; and women, in not showing enthusiasm for many aspects of it, are displaying resistance to participating in an institution which they do not have an equal part in creating.

And yet most men have believed that they were doing what a man 'should' by performing intercourse, and that a woman should orgasm from their thrusting. They were taught that providing a woman with intercourse, especially for an extended period of time, would give her what she wanted and needed. However, men have known on some level that it didn't, and this has led to deep, unspoken feelings of discomfort, alienation and guilt – which were often manifested as distrust of women's motives for having sex, and anger at women for not speaking up and being 'honest' about sex.

Where did the belief arise that women should orgasm from intercourse? The institution we know as 'sex' – 'foreplay' to intercourse ending with male orgasm – was first legislated into existence as the only acceptable form of sexual expression approximately 2,500 years ago, for purposes of increasing reproduction. But it did not take on the connotations we give it today until much later; intercourse was not always considered a romantic activity during which women were supposed to orgasm. In the late nineteenth century, in fact, women were considered vulgar if they did. However, in the early part of our century, with the increasing discussion of the rights of women, women's orgasm started to be considered important. Perhaps it seemed logical, in the beginning, to assume that women should orgasm from the same activity from which men orgasmed, especially since participation in this activity was glorified as being a form of 'natural law'. Of course, men orgasm from other forms of stimulation too, but the 'acceptable' time for men to orgasm was during intercourse.

If women formerly brought themselves to orgasm easily during masturbation, they have not felt free to explain the stimulation. In addition, women's interior clitoral anatomy had not yet been studied. However, it was known that women did masturbate to orgasm clitorally and generally not with vaginal penetration. Refusal to accept women's testimony on how they stimulated themselves was characteristic of the general attitude toward women as second-class citizen in a male-dominated society: women were advised to learn to orgasm 'the right way' – from vaginal penetration – and thus conform to supposed 'male sexuality' needs, women's role being that of 'helpmate'. When, however, this often did not work in practice, who was to blame? Who was flawed? Was it women or men – or both? Although generally it has been women who were considered inherently flawed or inadequate, in fact many men felt that they were to blame – that there was something deeply wrong with them or their penis when the woman did not orgasm. This oppressive expectation, then, has led to needless suffering, self-examination, and accusations between men and women.

Tragically, although most women have known how to stimulate themselves to orgasm easily during masturbation, they have not felt free to explain the stimulation they needed to men, or to stimulate themselves during sex with men. Being dependent on men, economically,[9] socially and politically, has kept women silent: women have not felt that they had the right to challenge the society's definition of sex or to assert their own needs and forms of sexual expression.

But on another level, women have been resistant to intercourse because intercourse has not been a choice. The legal structure in which women were owned by either their fathers or their husbands included (and still includes in many countries today) the provision that a man has a right to intercourse with his wife on demand; there was no such thing as rape in marriage. Further, many women have felt unable to protect themselves against pregnancy by using birth control, when it was against the rules of the state or church. Thus, in a very real sense, women had no rights over their own bodies, as their husbands controlled them; and therefore many women, feeling that their husbands could do with them whatever they pleased and that any attempt at resistance or influence was futile, developed very passive and hostile attitudes about sexual relationships: they would participate in sex but only when they had to and would not be any more active during it than necessary.

Thus intercourse, far from being a simple pleasurable activity, has for centuries symbolized and celebrated male domination and ownership of women, children and society. Conversely, it also symbolizes female subservience or being owned. A woman, in having intercourse, especially in the traditional position with the woman on the bottom, helping the man have an orgasm but not having one herself, was reminded of her position *vis-à-vis* the man. It is obvious, in this context, why many men would feel much more drawn toward participating in this institution than would women.

Many women's resistance to 'sex' – far from being simply negative 'conditioning' about sex – can also be seen as a large-scale and healthy resistance to being dominated and to their bodies being owned. Saying no to 'sex' has become, for many women, a way of maintaining dignity and integrity, together with some control over their own identity.

Today, women in some countries have the right to use birth control, but the forms available often make it difficult or dangerous; furthermore, the tradition of women's availability to men for orgasm inside the vagina is continued in the idea that the woman should have the entire responsibility for using birth control and that she should use a form which does not interfere with the man's pleasure – invisible, if possible. As one man remarked: 'Why, in all the movies or sex magazines, don't they ever show the problem of birth control? They make it too romantic.'

A basic cause of many women's resistance to sexual intercourse is emotional alienation. If women feel that men think of them as second-class and value them only as 'helpmates' and sexual partners, this is likely to lead to emotional alienation within the relationship – giving yet more cause for women's passive resistance (as defined by Gandhi) to having sex. One man embodied these attitudes quite clearly: 'My wife is not perhaps the woman one might dream up, but she's steady, dependable and consistent. She's the mother of my four kids, and in my own way I love her, even though she doesn't like sex too much. She doesn't initiate oral sex spontaneously, or intercourse either. She says the reason is because I don't show her enough kindness and affection throughout the day. She says if I did she'd be more active sexually. These things

47

are now so bad that I can't live with them, but after twenty-seven years of marriage, they bug me if I don't watch out.'

Another man commented on men's actions: 'Most men are only attentive to women when they want sex, and women know it. From my experience as a minister listening to married women describe their sexual problems, men spend their time, energy and interest elsewhere – then expect the women to want them when it's time for sex. This hurts the women considerably.'

This emotional alienation can be directly traced to the inequality created by the society in giving men rights and privileges over women and is aggravated by bringing up men and women with different psychological attitudes and rewarding them for different types of behaviour. Owning (or having the tradition of owning) women can lead men to have attitudes of condescension toward women while valuing other men more. But if a woman is valued only sexually, withholding sex can be her only power. If a man only expresses a real desire to spend time with a woman when he wants her to have sex with him, is it any wonder that a woman often says no? In a society in which women are dependent on men and in which men sometimes seem only to need women for sex, saying 'no' is many women's only chance to gain recognition as an individual or have some control in the relationship.

As one man put it: 'As a male, there is no question, we are always in control once she consents to lovemaking. We have the dick, that's all there is to it! We are the fucker and she is the fuckee. At the same time, in this society, the woman has the final choice as to sex or no sex. She can deny us (and herself) or she can engage in sex.'

How do men feel about all of this? Men often feel very angry with women who never initiate sex and too often don't want sex. But this anger has an undertone of alienation, guilt and insecurity: men feel instinctively on some level that sex does not involve an equal sharing, especially when they are having an orgasm and the woman does not – and this puts them on the defensive. As one man remarked: 'I feel more respect for her and myself if I don't feel I am cheating her of an orgasm – or I guess the word is "using" her, since I have an orgasm and she doesn't. I feel relieved to be with an equal.' But many men covered this feeling over by bragging, accepting their 'aggressiveness' as inherently 'male' and insisting that they were only behaving as their 'natures' compelled them to.

Although many men are very angry with women and suffer profound discomfort due to women's 'passivity' regarding sex – possibly because of buried feelings of guilt and defensiveness, knowing that somehow women are being exploited – most men do not overtly connect this with the need for improving women's status. Most men prefer to think that the problem is simply a lingering vestige of 'Victorian' morality – and further to believe that somehow women can be sexually 'free' even though they are not also economically and politically free.

Men are encouraged to accept this 'difference' between men and women and not to question it. Although many men instinctively feel uneasy on some level about what is going on, they are told by society that this is 'just the way things are'. Even though many men feel that by their having an orgasm and the woman not, they are exploiting the woman, that the situation is unfair or that the woman is somehow in an inferior position, they are told that it is men's 'nature' to continue wanting intercourse and having orgasm and that whether the woman does or not is 'her own problem'. Men's reaction to this is often to become alienated from women, to feel superior, uncomfortable, hostile or insecure with them. But, they may still wonder, do women really accept their less privileged status, or are women angry?

Men are faced with the dilemma of either believing that (1) women are built differently than men and do not always need orgasm to be satisfied and further that women in fact do not mind simply helping the man have an orgasm while they do not, or (2) that women can indeed orgasm (through masturbation, for example) but that they have been oppressed economically and socially into a position in which they have been forced to accede to men's wishes in sex, and that women have a hidden residue of anger at men for this. In other words, either women are innately unequal or women have been forced to submit. These are not pleasant options from which men may choose. If a man believes the first proposition, he must accept the idea that women are somehow fundamentally different from men in their basic humanity. This point of view was implied by Freud's famous question 'What do women want?' which seemed to say that what women want is so fundamentally different from what men want that it is mysterious and unfathomable. If a man accepts this, then his ability to be truly close to a woman is quite limited, as he feels himself so different from her.[10] Their relationship may be quite distant and formal, as each views the other as truly 'other'. On the other hand, if a man believes the second proposition, he is in a much better position for achieving a close and fulfilling relationship with a woman, even though he may have to re-examine how sexuality is defined and rethink the basis of male-female relationships. But this process can lead to much greater fulfilment and happiness for a man in his own sexuality and life.

1   See measurements of the contractions and other physical responses conducted by Masters & Johnson, 1966

2   Books related to this subject include *Egypt and Chaldea* by W. Boscawen (London: Harper, 1894); *Ancient Israel*, by Roland DeVaux (London: Darton, Longman & Todd, 1965); *The Lost World of Elan* by Walther Hint (New York: New York University Press, 1973); *The Splendour That Was Egypt* by Margaret Murray (London: Sidgwick & Jackson, 1949); *When God Was a Woman* by Merlin Stone (New York: Dial Press, 1976); and *Prehistory and the Beginning of Civilization* by Jacquetta Hawkes and Sir Leonard Woolley. Also helpful is the extensive bibliography contained in *When God Was a Woman*.

3   See Jane Harrison, *Prologomena to the Study of Greek Religion*, Cambridge, 1903; and E. A. Butterworth, *Some Traces of the Pre-Olympian World*, Berlin and New York, De Cruyter, 1966.

4   However, women then, as today, must have known about the importance of the clitoris since, as discussed in *The Hite Report on Female Sexuality*, women in the twentieth century, without being given any information whatsoever on how, begin to masturbate quite early in their lives. For the great majority of women this has meant manual clitoral stimulation. Therefore it is logical to assume that if women do this 'instinctively' today, women must also have done this then and known that this was a pleasurable area to have stimulated. Was this sublimation part of sexual institutions or customs at that time? Was masturbation considered private? What other activities were considered important?

5   These laws may have stemmed from certain Indo-European or Aryan ideologies: the same ideologies which influenced early religion in Iran, Turkey and India.

6   Most of these societies also had early non-patriarchal traditions which are just beginning to be studied and understood.

7   If coitus is really the basic expression of men's 'sex drive', why does society need so many laws and religious injunctions to insist that this is the only 'right' way for them to have sex?

8   Although a minority of women do orgasm during intercourse itself, as they explain in *The Hite Report on Female Sexuality*, this is most often due to friction between the two pubic areas or other such exterior contact, which can sometimes accompany penetration.

9   For example, the US 1980 census report showed that still, for every $1.00 a man makes, a woman makes only $0.59 for equal work. This gap has been evident and continues to be in US Bureau of Labor statistics until the present, 2005. The amount women earn proportionate to men is universally lower.

10   Not only sexually, but also in what he wants out of life; he may feel he is more aggressive and demanding of life in general, in his career, etc., than women – who are 'naturally' content with home and security. This can make men feel alienated, emotionally unconnected, isolated, or angry.

Chapter Four

Women and Orgasm: Men's Experiences

Requiem for the G-Spot

My research indicates that, rather than the 'G-spot', it is the clitoris – or 'C-spot', as I propose to call it – that is most important for women. Yet the 'vaginal orgasm' tried to make a comeback under a trendy-sounding new name in the 1980s when the idea was floated into the media that women have an interior 'G-spot' inside the vagina that causes orgasm if stimulated in the proper way. A new version of the old 'vaginal orgasm' idea, thus removing once again the need for 'extra clitoral stimulation': how convenient! Yet has it worked?

If the so-called 'G-spot' were so effective, rather than being just a contemporary apology for the status quo, why haven't more women been having orgasms for centuries during coitus? Why don't more women masturbate by insertion trying to touch themselves inside the vagina instead of caressing their pubic and clitoral areas, as they do? Clearly women are voting with their actions.

The notion of a G-spot has now been debunked by researchers in several countries from Australia to Canada to Italy.

The theory that women have an interior 'G-spot' inside the vagina that causes orgasm if stimulated in the proper way became popular in the late 1970s when three clinical researchers published a book based on scanty research, asserting that one of the interior walls of the vagina contains a spot or interior point that, when contacted, stimulates female orgasm. The letter 'G' stands for one Dr Grafenberg, by then deceased. The researchers did not explain why this 'spot' had not led to orgasm for the great majority of women for centuries but simply asserted that there is such a thing – thus resuscitating the belief that orgasm 'should' occur with vaginal stimulation, rather than exterior clitoral stimulation, in 'the normal woman'.

Although there has been much talk in the media of this G-spot, so that people have consequently had ample time to try finding and contacting this 'point' to cause orgasm during intercourse, no research shows an increase in rate of orgasm during intercourse without the use of stimulation of the mons-clitoral area; indeed, research in the US in 2004 shows that one out of three women 'have difficulty' having orgasm with their partners and quickly become tired of sex. This could be avoided if women's new thinking about sex and orgasm were allowed to flourish, rather than the media versions of it. Additionally, it has been common knowledge for at least a century that women have 'difficulty' reaching orgasm during simple coitus; why would this have been true if an interior spot were capable of causing orgasm in women? If there had been a physiological G-spot, it would have proved effective for female orgasm all along.

Between 1999 and 2001 research in several countries found that no such spot exists. In other words, research indicates that it is the 'C-spot' or clitoris, rather than the 'G-spot' that is most important for women. In fact, most women need separate stimulation or massage of this area external to the vagina in order to fully orgasm – thus implying that sex should develop a new focus. After all, if the G-spot were effective, then why haven't more women been having orgasms for centuries during coitus when the spot was supposedly contacted? Why don't more women masturbate by insertion to touch themselves inside the vagina, aiming for this spot instead of caressing their pubic and clitoral areas as they do?

For many, hasn't looking for a theoretical spot inside the vagina simply been a way of putting off making the changes in sexual relations being called for by women? Isn't insisting that there is a mysterious 'spot' inside the vagina only a way of continuing an outworn definition of sex, and pushing women, as in the past, to 'find their vaginal destiny'? Clearly women are voting with their actions. Women have a right to clitoral or exterior pubic stimulation to orgasm during sex with a partner. This is part of the broader movement for women's rights and part of the changing society around us. This is not to say that the vagina is not highly erotic and sensitive or that it cannot bring intense satisfaction to a woman with the right partner: there is something very symbolic about being 'penetrated' by another, as men too can experience. Women do feel highly charged sexual sensations during coitus, although the stimulation is usually not the kind that leads to orgasm. The vast majority of women can masturbate easily to one or more orgasms by simply placing their hand or fingers externally on their bodies, caressing the clitoris and mons area of their vulva, sometimes lower. This type of stimulation can be built into the sexual scenario between two people, as it already is between women who have sex together. Although certainly some men – especially during the last two decades – have learned to appreciate this, no such type of activity to orgasm has ever been shown in any Hollywood film, which often imply a couple will have or is having intercourse. The constant glamorizing of the vagina (and feelings inside the vagina) as opposed to the clitoris means that many people want to believe there is a 'G-spot' – probably so that they won't have to change. For almost every woman, masturbation is clitoral and exterior to the vulva. Women, not having been taught by society how to masturbate and thus simply discovering their bodies' feelings and needs, usually as girls, indicate with their choice of stimulation during masturbation how they most easily orgasm. The definition of sex that is now evolving should reflect this reality. If the G-spot were an important reality for most women, at least some women would masturbate by contacting it, not by exterior stimulation, or would at least use this internal stimulation (touching or stroking this part of their vagina with their finger or an object) to enhance stimulation during clitoral masturbation. Neither is the case. This does not mean that women do not enjoy or seek intercourse and 'vaginal penetration'(or 'penile covering'). This is one of the complexities of sexual desire: for many women, coitus or vaginal penetration is an extremely pleasurable part of 'foreplay', bringing them to a high pitch of arousal, although they then want clitoral stimulation to orgasm to follow this 'coital foreplay'.

Redefining Sex

Society has long known that it is easier for women to orgasm during masturbation than coitus – and that masturbation is clitoral and exterior, not vaginal. Yet the society condemned women, as if their feelings were wrong, incorrect. In the twentieth century, although both Freud and Kinsey knew that women could orgasm much more easily with clitoral stimulation than vaginal penetration, both failed to draw a logical conclusion, continuing to present theories claiming that women were somehow at fault! Instead of seeing that society was oppressing women, they expected women to change; Freud believed women should grow up to 'adjust' and become 'mature', while Kinsey thought that when a woman had been married longer, had more experience sexually, she would achieve this result.

The trendy sound of the 'G-spot' should not fool people into believing that coitus, having failed to bring women to orgasm for decades, would suddenly do the trick. Women need stimulation of the C-spot all the way to orgasm!

It is the definition of sex that should change, not women's bodies. Are women now redefining sexuality? Women are making many changes in how they see and practice intimate physical relations – how they express and share their bodies. Although the choices are theirs, really theirs, it can still take some time to wake up and see that one is free, in charge of one's life, that all decisions are possible; like Sleeping Beauty awaking, after 2,000 years of misinformation women need a little time to think clearly.

Unfortunately, women are currently encouraged to be 'active' in male ways, rather than their own – for example, performing actions that demonstrate intercourse is making them more and more excited (may or may not be true), 'initiating' sexual activities long defined to be 'sexual' by men, 'acting hot' wearing 'sexy' shocking outfits, etc. In reality, being active in sex has an entirely different meaning for women, a meaning that is only beginning to unfold. For example, if women know how to reach orgasm on their own during masturbation, why don't they touch themselves in the same way during sex with a partner and make themselves orgasm? Many women say that the men they know do not expect this, and so do not aid in this process, perhaps by touching them or whispering words of encouragement – although they hope that this will change any day now.

The semi-pornographic images of women visible on so many advertising posters and in television commercials – these same images that are sometimes used by fundamentalists to point to 'the decadence of the secular West' or 'the shameful lack of values in today's society' – do not represent who women are sexually but rather the use and selling of women's bodies by a commercial double standard. It is no wonder, with female sexuality equated with what is shown in many ads, that some women today recoil, deciding 'the old ways' were best, imagining that women were more respected then – whether or not this is historically accurate – and embrace a traditionalist version of religion and family values. One of the keys to female sexuality during the next hundred years, I am sure, will be that women will begin initiating a new type of sexuality – something that will cause a real revolution in sexuality, one that has as yet barely begun – despite all the courageous changes people have made in their sexual behaviour and private lives. Women may have hardly begun to show who they are sexually.

Built-In 'Inadequacy' for Men in the Current Definition of Sex

A constant source of anxiety among men is whether they continue intercourse long enough, remaining erect, or whether they reach orgasm 'too soon'. Most men, although they sometimes used the term 'premature ejaculation', did not in fact refer to its standard clinical meaning – i.e., orgasm before or just at the moment of penetration – but rather referred to very varied amounts of time of intercourse. In fact, most men who expressed this concern felt that this was probably the reason why a woman might not reach orgasm during intercourse with them. This thinking is inaccurate, however, as discussed in *The Hite Report on Female Sexuality*.

Seventy-four percent of the men who answered that research project expressed concern over whether they continued intercourse long enough: 'Sadly, so far, I have been climaxing too soon to suit me. I can't control it. And I feel as though I haven't really done much for my partner even though I do try to continue stimulation somehow. I consider it a failed test of virility.'

The popular media are constantly warning men against 'coming too soon', insisting that this is the cause of most woman not having orgasm from coitus. Thus most men feel it is their duty to the woman to have intercourse for as long as possible, so that the woman can have a chance to orgasm too. However, the results of *The Hite Report on Female Sexuality* suggest that this is a fallacy, since whether a woman has an orgasm is usually not related to length of intercourse. In fact, most women do not orgasm simply as a result of intercourse; and the minority of women who do, do so not so much from long- thrusting as from individually created ways of getting specific clitoral stimulation during intercourse.

But the amount of pressure on men has been enormous. Even the term 'premature ejaculation' is negative, giving a man the implicit message that no matter when he orgasms it may be too soon, 'premature', unwanted or out of place. Men have been getting a double message: on the one hand they are told that it is very 'virile' to become erect and excited and thrust home to orgasm; on the other hand, they are told not to orgasm 'too soon'. Since most men get rather good stimulation during thrusting, this provides a contradiction – leaving most men feeling slightly uneasy, guilty and inadequate.

Although extending intercourse can be a pleasure in itself for both men and women, this guilt is unnecessary – as long as women's needs are acknowledged in a realistic manner at some time during sex or any special needs of women desiring to orgasm during intercourse are fulfilled in a mutually agreeable fashion.

Penis Size

It seems that men in their twenties today are still as worried about penis size as men have been for a long time. A young man (age eighteen) writes me with great sincerity, 'There is a problem. My girlfriend reaches orgasm when I masturbate her or I practice oral sex on her but not with penetration. She feels frustrated, because all her friends can have an orgasm that way – and I worry that the problem could be my penis size; I am in erection 20 cm tall and 12 cm around.'

Although this cliché was overturned in the 1960s and reburied again later, it seems to have made a dramatic comeback. Discussions of the drug Viagra have added to the presumption on the part of the very young that 'everybody knows' a man should have 'a big hard one'.

Many young men also have a prejudice that lingers about practicing C-spot stimulation with their female partners. As one puts it: 'I understand that some women cannot reach orgasm with penetration, but I want to try to make them happy.' In what he thinks is an understanding statement, by his choice of words he has already put any female partner he might have on the defensive! First, he implies that only 'some women' have this 'lack of capacity', thus they are 'incapable', 'not like the others' and so on. In other words, they are 'not as good as the others'.

Rather than accept the happy reality of how most women reach orgasm, being happy about the diversity offered, sharing that and changing the shape of 'sex', some men worry about whether or not they have the right penis size: i.e., whether or not they are 'big enough'. The supposition is: 'I'm sure that if I were big enough, she would have orgasm during penetration – just like in the porno movies!' Is it penis size such men are worried about, or fear of learning the 'ins and outs' of clitoral stimulation?

Maybe it is natural for a man – when he finds that life is different than he has been told it will be, that his girlfriend has an orgasm easily with stimulation by hand but not via coitus, although his friends say their experiences are different, their girlfriends always have orgasms – to have doubts. It is natural at this stage in our history that people would be filled with doubts. After all, for how many centuries has it been said that sex should happen in one particular way? For a very long time. We are on the cutting edge of a new society, and it takes courage to live one's life authentically, believe in oneself and in one's partner.

An insistence on focusing on erection does a terrible disservice to both men and women. Any man who finds himself thinking something like this should ask himself if he believes that he has been brainwashed by imposed beliefs about 'having a hard penis' – or if he really is speaking about his own pleasure in feeling excited when he has an erection. Feeling the pleasure of one's own body is clearly the right of every human being; being brainwashed by slogans that are not good for you or your partner is another.

Pressure to 'Make Her Come'

Closely linked with the traditional pressure on men to maintain a long erection and thrusting during intercourse is the idea that it is a man's role to 'give' the woman an orgasm during intercourse. Just as the man has traditionally been considered the 'provider' economically – the man should 'bring home the bacon' or buy the house – he has also been given the role of 'providing' the woman with sexual satisfaction. A 'real man' should 'make her come'.

In addition to the pressure created by this role, this idea also often puts the man in a no-win situation since the information he has been given – that thrusting during intercourse should bring a woman to orgasm – is faulty. This places him in a vulnerable position, leaving him to doubt his masculinity whenever female orgasm does not occur and also possibly pressuring the woman to fake orgasms. Thus this needless pressure alienates men and women, as each blames the other when expectations are not met.

When asked 'Do you feel there is something wrong with your "performance", technique, or sensitivity if the woman does not orgasm from intercourse itself? That you're "not man enough"?' a few men insisted women never fail to orgasm with them:

'Are you kidding? I never had a complaint. I never have failed a woman yet to achieve orgasm.'

'Experience has shown that if a woman can't orgasm with me, she can't with anybody. I have brought out the first orgasm in several.'

But the overwhelming majority of men realized that women often did not orgasm during intercourse and found this a source of pressure. Many felt it was their fault: 'If anything goes wrong, I'm blamed for it. Girls always seem to just lay there and say, "OK, make it happen." I feel an immense pressure to perform and feel that it's all up to me.'

This pressure to orgasm from intercourse has been very oppressive to women and has often led to faking orgasms. And, in fact, although men here say that they do not feel guilty, there is a tone of defensiveness. The unrealistic goal of women reaching orgasm simply from the rubbing of the penis in the vagina has placed undue pressure on both men and women, and left both vulnerable and defensive before each other – creating, all too often, an adversary situation.

Doubts, Questions and Lack of Information About Women's Orgasms

What is the cause of women's seeming lack of interest in sex? Of what many men called women's 'passivity' during sex? Certainly it is not any innate biological difference from men in desire for orgasm[1] or desire for closeness and touching. Nor is it, for the most part, 'Victorian upbringing,' although this was the reason usually ascribed to it by men. Nor is it related in older women to 'menopause', since this does not in any way reduce or end women's sexual feelings.

Let's look at one of the most obvious explanations: that is, that most women's need for specific (non-coital) clitoral stimulation to orgasm is frequently not recognized – so that many women never or only irregularly orgasm during sex with men. This cultural denial of women's sexual needs reflects the larger social system in which women have been given second-class status for hundreds of years and is part of a larger problem between men and women.

How has this affected men? How has women's lack of orgasm, or the irregularity of their orgasms, made men feel? How has it put pressures on men? Increased tensions between men and women? And how is this new information, and women's new possibly active role, being accepted and integrated – or not being integrated – into sex?

Most men who participated in this research stated that they had experienced a great deal of insecurity and confusion over knowing when – or whether – a woman had had an orgasm. An overwhelming majority of them were looking for this orgasm during intercourse. In fact, most men had great doubts about whether, or how frequently, women had orgasms with them; 61 percent of the men who answered said they usually could not tell when a woman had an orgasm or could not be sure.

Most men still assume women should orgasm from intercourse and lack information about the clitoris:

'I always assumed there was something wrong with them if they couldn't orgasm with each intercourse without clitoral stimulation. That prejudice dies hard. Although now I know what the truth is, doubts still remain just below rational consciousness.'

'One weekend my wife sent the kids off to their grandparents' house, and then she told me she had something to tell me. Well, what it was was that she didn't have orgasms the way I thought she did, that she didn't mean to hurt me, that she had really loved having sex with me all those years, but she just hadn't been honest. I was flabbergasted, I didn't know what to say. We started talking and she told me just how she did orgasm, and then I couldn't believe my eyes, she showed me how she did it. I have never been the same since, I mean for the better. I fell in love with her all over again, or anyway, I got a case of the hots for her that didn't quiet down for about six months. She was much more interested in sex than before. I learned how to make her come with my hand and we started specializing in weekend-long sex sessions. It was just too much. Bliss. Heaven. I was ready to die.'

'When I first read that women needed stimulation on their clitoris and didn't usually orgasm with the penis, I thought, but what about all those women who had orgasms with me? Then I realized maybe they didn't really have orgasms, maybe they were just excited with me. I usually said something like "Was it good?" and they would say yeah – but maybe they didn't orgasm at all. That thought really shoots my ego down. Why don't they tell men? Why put men in such a stupid position? It made me feel like a fool, not knowing all those years and acting like such a big jock. Were the women laughing at me behind my back? Or feeling sorry for me, or thinking I was stupid? Did other men treat them different? It's all just too hard to believe.'

Sixty-one percent of the men in my study do not know, or are not sure, when a woman has an orgasm. Much of this uncertainty is due to the fact that men have wrongly been taught that woman should orgasm from the thrusting of the penis and have been told very little about clitoral stimulation and so are looking for women's orgasm at the wrong time. The fact is that only approximately 30 percent of women do orgasm from intercourse itself[2], usually from pubic area contact, rather than thrusting *per se*; on the other hand, most women orgasm easily from more direct clitoral stimulation.

In spite of this, most men still assume women should orgasm from simple thrusting during intercourse, and would greatly prefer that they do.

What Men Say about Women's Orgasms in My Research

Would you prefer to have sex with a woman who has orgasm from intercourse (coitus), rather than clitoral stimulation? Most men still assume women either should or would orgasm from simple intercourse (coitus)[3]:

'If she didn't come during intercourse I would wonder why she didn't.'

'Some women will not orgasm from intercourse. Either they do not know how to make themselves orgasm or they do not want to. I feel a woman should orgasm during intercourse. She should try all different positions till she finds one that is best for her. If a woman can have fantasies when she is having intercourse and learn how to enjoy each movement, she will find that she will orgasm. I have taught this to many women with good results. Of course, the man has to know how to fuck.'

'A lot of women have trouble reaching a climax. Some women should have surgery or go to a psychiatrist. I went with four women in a row that had to have manual stimulation to reach a climax. I was a little bit shaky, wondering if the entire sex had gone to pot.'

'I believe that a woman's emotions play a large part in whether she has an orgasm. If I am tender and careful to be attentive to her during intercourse and still she doesn't have an orgasm, then the problem is in her head. She either doesn't love me enough or is preoccupied with something that's bothering her or something. If she wants to be orgasmic, I believe that a woman can be.'

And the overwhelming majority of men preferred the woman to orgasm from coitus:

'I prefer to have sex with a woman who orgasms from intercourse to a woman who only orgasms from clitoral stimulation.'

'I like it if she gets off when I do; I feel like that is the most 'natural' and free way for me.'

Answers seen here include men of all ages, points of view and backgrounds; younger and older men alike were just as likely to expect women to orgasm from intercourse and to be unfamiliar with giving clitoral stimulation to orgasm:

'I prefer intercourse because during intercourse you get the idea that you're both thoroughly involved at the same time.'

'Coitus, because I want to feel her orgasm on my penis. Also, I think her orgasm would be more violent and all-encompassing.'

An almost equally large number answered 'either' or 'both'. Often they included the phrases 'I don't care how she has orgasms – either way', or 'it doesn't matter to me how she does it', or 'any way she wants to'. These statements seemed to indicate less a willingness to try anything than a kind of lack of knowledge or frustration with the 'problem' of women's orgasms. Perhaps it was easier for these men to say something like 'it doesn't matter to me as long as she gets pleasure' than to really distinguish what it is their partners specifically require:

'It doesn't really matter – any way they want to get off is fine with me.'

'I have only had intercourse with my wife. I don't care how she has orgasm, she can have it any way she wants to. If my wife wants to stimulate herself with a freight train she has my blessing. But if my wife does not orgasm during intercourse I do not feel bad. In fact, I like it better when she does not orgasm because she will be warmer next time. She is best when she orgasms about once a week.'

'I enjoy the freedom of stimulation in any manner. I dislike any limitations.'

'I don't really prefer any certain way for the woman to get off. I don't think that much about whether she is getting off but I do what I can to make the experience the most exhilarating for the both of us.'

'It doesn't matter to me. I prefer to have sex with women that are sexually uninhibited, with open minds, and have clear thoughts about themselves and their sexuality.

And several men said they would prefer 'both' – as long as her orgasm during intercourse was the grand finale:

'I prefer a woman who has both. The best times are when I can create at least a couple of clitoral orgasms before we begin to have intercourse and then be able to make her climax vaginally three or four times.'

'The woman who has orgasm first from clitoral, then again during intercourse with my orgasm is the best.'

However, some men who gave 'both' as their answer indicated a more complete understanding of the alternatives:

'Sometimes I would prefer to have her orgasm from intercourse rather than from clitoral stimulation, but not always. It's a different sort of enjoyment. When she orgasms from intercourse, I have to exercise more self-discipline. However, it does cause contractions in her vagina, which give me a good deal of pleasure, as well as her body movements just prior to orgasm. But if she orgasms from clitoral stimulation, I can then fuck at my own speed knowing that she is not depending on me to last a certain length of time. Also when she has her orgasm prior to my entry, it makes her very loose and slippery and sensual, which I like.'

'I don't feel it is very important whether the woman has orgasm from intercourse or clitoral stimulation. Most of the women I have known have had orgasms more readily and apparently with as much pleasure, from clitoral stimulation. I get a big kick out of stimulating a woman to orgasm with my hand. Orgasm during actual intercourse is also nice. If I stimulate a woman with my hand during sex, it often is the case that the woman can experience more than one orgasm. If she only has orgasm during intercourse, it often excites me to the point of orgasm too, and the woman then has less chance of multiple orgasms, my potential for frequent orgasms being very small.'

Many men avoided answering this question directly, often discussing the importance of feelings, while ignoring the issue of how the woman actually did orgasm:

'The partner's type of stimulation is not as important as that there be mutual physical satisfaction and love.'

'I'm one of those fools who links sex and love as much as possible – in other words, I try just to make love to women I care a lot about – so giving a woman an orgasm is more important than the process of doing so. In summation of all this, I really don't have a preference.'

'I prefer to have sex with a woman who has knowledge of how to stimulate me and no hang-ups about any part of her own anatomy.'

'The question is whether she had pleasure from going to bed with me and not whether she had an orgasm.'

Others expressed confusion over whether intercourse itself actually provides indirect clitoral stimulation for the woman:

'Why separate orgasm from intercourse from orgasm from clitoral stimulation? Can't coitus also stimulate the clitoris? I do not really have a preference anyway – I want to give a woman what she wants, and as I observe orgasm, I can't tell any difference. Nearly all women can orgasm from finger/tongue stimulation directly to the clitoris. Some have a very hard time reaching orgasm from straight coitus.'

'I try to have my woman get off first during foreplay, then intercourse; both are clitoral stimulation just by different means – or am I mistaken? If they have an orgasm at all, I'm happy.'

'Aren't they the same? Isn't that question settled yet?'

Or held the misconception that it did:

'I believe clitoral stimulation is the only way a woman can reach orgasm. What most people feel is coital stimulation is really a very gentle and indirect clitoral stimulation.'

A few men used the phrase 'She gets clitoral stimulation from my penis' with no explanation given as to what the writer meant or as to how this might be true – implying a possible misunderstanding of female anatomy:

'During intercourse I never had a woman stimulate herself other than to rub her clitoris against my inserted penis.'

Women in *The Hite Report on Female Sexuality* who had an orgasm during intercourse without the addition of manual clitoral stimulation usually got the needed clitoral stimulation from friction on their mons, in contact with the man's pubic area, and not from simple thrusting inside the vagina, as these testimonies reveal:

'I believe that a woman who has coitus orgasm can be easier stimulated to orgasm than one who has clitoral orgasm because of the location of the penis in the vaginal tract.'

'Standing up against a wall allows the woman to get more stimulation of her clitoris. As the penis goes into the vagina the outer lips are pulled down and in slightly. This allows the swollen clitoris to contact the top of the penis and thereby stimulate the woman. However, if the woman is shorter than the man, he must either bend slightly at the knees, or she must stand in a little higher on some support.'

'All orgasms are from the clitoris. My penis comes in consistent contact with my wife's clitoris so she's really getting clitoral stimulation as part of our intercourse.'

However, the fact that these methods can work for some women in some situations does not imply that all women 'should' be able to make them work. For example, a great many women can orgasm only with their legs and thighs together. Most men who had done clitoral stimulation clearly thought of the clitoris as something there to fall back on if nothing else worked; for a woman to have an orgasm from clitoral stimulation was second best. Many also said, surprisingly, that they would still prefer the woman to orgasm from coitus – even though this was not the case or would be impossible!

Other men, however, clearly expressed that – since it is the woman's anatomy! – it is the woman, not the man, who has the right to a preference:

'Whatever my wife wants is best. She's what I want.'

'I love whatever she loves. I love her, not a "type" of woman who orgasms from one thing or another.'

'No preferences. You have to find what each woman prefers. I would simply adjust.'

'Her choice.'

A few men do say that clitoral stimulation is necessary and they enjoy it:

'Clitoral stimulation is enjoyable because I can be 100 percent aware of what is happening to her – preceding, during, and after her orgasm – without having my orgasm distract me from my attention to her.'

'I enjoy stimulating the clitoris and bringing on orgasm manually.'[4]

There was a tendency in some of the answers to this question to hope or assume, if the respondent was aware of the statistics of *The Hite Report on Female Sexuality*, that his partner was among the 30 percent of women who do get clitoral stimulation during intercourse (adequate to orgasm) – and a further tendency to believe that the most 'mature' and 'best' women are naturally among the 30 percent.

Some men told how they had felt when they first realized that, contrary to cultural stereotypes, clitoral stimulation was more important for most women's orgasms than intercourse itself – that intercourse did not actually lead to orgasm for most women:

'I used to think I understood feminine sexuality – you know, I was gentle, patient, understanding, etc. – if they "couldn't" orgasm, it was "OK", I let them get on top during intercourse and everything (a real sport, wasn't

I?). Anyway, now I see that the sensitivity I had that I thought was about 90 percent was more like 10 percent.' (Age twenty-two.)

'I guess I had personally observed in my own experience that the clitoris was the place of excitement in the female; I know that on many occasions I knocked myself out thrusting in the female with little effect. There was something wrong, but I must admit I was crestfallen when I finally became aware that what I had suspected was true – male thrusting of the penis in the female vagina is not what we males thought it was.' (Age thirty-eight.)

'I didn't feel good when I heard it. I didn't feel good for them, like a car with a defect that the dealer wouldn't fix. You're stuck with it and have to work around it. Or don't drive.' (Age thirty.)

'The other day a friend of mine told me that I was making a mistake expecting women to orgasm during intercourse with me, and that I should try to stimulate them some other way. This was radical news to me. It was odd, talking about it with another man like that. I have never really talked about sex with another man before, except the usual stories, etc. I wonder what he thought of my reaction, or if he thought I should have known or what. Anyway, I'm glad he told me.' (Age thirty-one.)

'Through almost eleven years of marriage, I believed that orgasm through intercourse was the rule rather than the exception. I "knew" that the clitoris was part of the female orgasm process – nothing more. In the last year a lover entered my life (I am still married) and it is with her and through reading *The Hite Report* that I began to understand the function of the clitoris and the importance of manual stimulation. It has opened up a whole new side of sexuality, an addition.' (Age forty.)

Certain men had accepted the information with relief and a sense of pleasure – especially when it confirmed their own personal experience or when they thought that the 'problem' had been their fault:

'My wife has never orgasmed from intercourse. I used to feel that something was wrong with my technique or with my wife's frame of mind (mental block).

Now all that is gone and forgotten. She can always orgasm from clitoral stimulation, so we are not missing something.' (Age forty-six.)

'I can't believe we have been deceived so long about the penis-vagina orgasm. I am sure my wife (and I) would have developed much more sensibly if we had known this fact thirty-five years ago. I often felt sad and puzzled that she did not orgasm from intercourse. I was relieved to find out that this is normal.' (Age fifty-seven.)

One man had worried at first that the news that women needed more clitoral stimulation would mean even more work for him, and even more pressure to perform ('give the woman an orgasm'):

'At first I was worried because I thought this would mean more responsibility for me, that women needed more stimulation, not that it would make things easier in the long run. But that's how it worked out, really, because I don't have to strain so much during intercourse for a result that's impossible anyway – and besides, sometimes she helps me with her hand on top of mine stimulating her clitoris. I'm glad I learned.' (Age forty-six.)

Some men voiced the difficulties of changing:

'I feel a great resistance in myself to the idea that a woman really needs direct clitoral or mons stimulation to orgasm. She should be able to orgasm during intercourse – that is what men have always said. And yet, if it isn't true, it isn't true. I know I should accept it, but it's really a revolutionary change in all my assumptions (and the way I've always behaved). I have to force myself to believe it. And yet, how egotistical can I be, with my very own love telling me it is so? Change is hard.'

'It's a bit worrying to think of women not enjoying intercourse as we do – hope they're not going to lock us out of their vaginas forever. Still, the facts of female physiology can't be denied, even if they're not as men might wish. As Martin Luther declared: "There I stand. I can do no other."'

One man was grappling with the information and its implications – wondering how the woman felt about intercourse and how he himself should feel about it – and in the process rethinking his own definition of sex:

'First of all my partner, my wife, has never orgasmed during intercourse, or in my presence, while nearly every time we have had intercourse, I have come to orgasm and ejaculation. Never! Here is the way I feel about it. Besides expecting to orgasm during sexual intercourse, I rejoice in the fact that I can orgasm during intercourse. I consider orgasm during masturbation and during intercourse as two different types of orgasm: masturbatory orgasm, for me, is a selfish orgasm, a self-love orgasm, all for myself. Orgasm during intercourse, to me, is a mutual orgasm, that is, I feel that I have not brought myself to "come", but also that my wife has helped me to "come". The fact I am enjoying the physical contact and closeness with her, the fact she has allowed me to penetrate her, make love to her, is an intricate/intimate articulation of the fact my orgasm is in part a gift from her. To me, emotionally and psychologically, this is ultimate, this kind of orgasm means so much more to me than my own masturbatory orgasm. This is how I feel I am.'

'But I feel bothered I cannot bring her to orgasm during a mutual experience of lovemaking and intercourse. I do not feel bothered because I feel responsible to bring her to "come", or that "it is my job". I have transcended this expectation. She is entitled to her orgasms as I am (masturbatorily). But, because I feel so much ecstasy when I have come while having coitus with her, I feel that I can be a part of an orgasm with her. I want to give or bring her to orgasm. Can you sympathize or empathize with me? When I come and she does not, I feel one-sided about the orgasmic ecstasy: I feel I have reached a plateau she has not, which does make me feel alone in ecstasy, sometimes lonely. I desire my body, myself and my lovemaking to be in part hers, for her, the gift of myself to her.'

'As for helping my wife (if she wants it) to come before or after I come, I feel all game and willing to participate in this. But she feels a bit embarrassed to stimulate herself "in front of me". This is OK. What I wish to make clear is that I am quite willing to help her come, in whatever manner it takes.'

A popular response was to say that the woman's orgasm is her own responsibility:

'It's her business. She is responsible for her own orgasms.'

'I offer everything, if she doesn't accept, I'm clean.'

'The problem would be more hers than mine. She needs to know what turns her on.'

'It's not my problem. It's up to her.'

'I consider myself ultimately responsible for providing my own orgasms. To be hard-nosed about it, I frankly consider a woman ultimately responsible for hers too. None of my relationships has ever been so lacking in respect, tenderness and diplomacy that we degenerated to fighting about orgasms, but if it didn't happen, and I was accused of "being not man enough", I would counter righteously that it takes two, and it is more than likely that she wasn't woman enough.'

These answers are certainly correct in one sense – that everyone does, finally, make his or her own orgasm. However, a woman's situation is different from that of a man. To imply that women are not taking their fair share of responsibility for what goes on overlooks the fact that most 'sex is still carried on according to the old rules – that is, the woman is supposed to orgasm from intercourse, intercourse is sex, it is assumed that intercourse will be included and that the man has the right to the appropriate stimulation for his orgasm, i.e., intercourse. The man has society behind him, encouraging him to have his orgasm, but the woman has society telling her that what she needs – i.e., clitoral stimulation to orgasm, usually in the form of manual or oral stimulation – is not 'normal', or that she has no right to assert herself. In other words, our pattern of sex does not put men in the position of having to ask for the stimulation they need; it is clear that 'sex' should end with intercourse and male orgasm, whereas women must request 'special' ('extra') stimulation and/or stimulation not related to intercourse. As one man put it: 'If the woman needs some special stimulation, she should let the guy know.'

In summary, many men were very annoyed with women for not having orgasms more frequently or more easily during sex – feeling 'Why are women being so difficult? They could orgasm if they wanted to, if they would just try a little harder, or if they were not being overly emotionally complicated – why are they trying to make men feel bad?' – not realizing that it is the lack of adequate clitoral stimulation in traditional 'sex' that makes orgasm difficult for most women, and not esoteric reasons. There was a great sense of annoyance, anger, and hostility in these answers – why are women so difficult after all?

'Women Should Speak Up'

Other men felt the situation was the woman's fault in the sense that the woman should tell the man what she needs – and should especially speak up about her need for clitoral stimulation outside of intercourse – although here again, many answers seemed still to imply that the woman would speak up about some particular preferences during intercourse. Men were frequently angry if they felt women wouldn't tell them what they wanted:

'There is something wrong with me only if a woman lets me know that she can orgasm if I do a certain thing, and I refuse to do it. Nothing works all the time for everyone, and I'm not going to stake my manhood on my ability to read minds.'

'I would prefer she would tell me anything she wants rather than dead silence.'

'It's her fault. I'm not a mind reader. She has to tell me what to do.'

'I would help, if she would just tell me. It really pisses me off to think that a girl would tell me she had come when she hadn't and wanted to. Hell, that's what I'm there for!'

'I wish I knew what they were scared of. I assume that if she's not satisfied she'll tell me. But again, just try to find a woman this open – I think it's almost impossible. This is why I'm sick and tired of women's libbers telling everybody that men just like to "love 'em and leave 'em". This is bullshit. The truth is that women avoid being controlled by men by being secretive and unpredictable.'

Feelings of Alienation and Anger

How do you feel if the woman you are with does not have an orgasm at all in any way?
Doubts about how or if women were having orgasms frequently made men feel uncomfortable, guilty, inadequate or defensive during sex – although some men said that they didn't care whether a woman had orgasms or not, since women's orgasms were not that important. But most men, still assuming women should orgasm during intercourse, all too often wound up feeling alienated,

either blaming themselves or blaming women for not achieving what really is very difficult or impossible to achieve:

'How do I feel? Like a doctor who loses a patient on the surgery table.'

'Inadequate, a poor lover, a failure.'

'Depressed, disappointed. Feelings of self-hatred.'

'She says it's OK, but I worry.'

'A selfish pig. There's no point in making love.'

'With my first wife, I became indifferent.'

'I feel parasitic or unexciting.'

'I would lose interest in her.'

Lack of women's orgasm, mainly due to cultural imperatives that insist women should orgasm when men do, has been an unspoken source of alienation between men and women over the years. As one man put it: 'I feel more respect for her and myself if I don't feel I am cheating her out of an orgasm – or I guess the word is "using" her, since I have an orgasm and she doesn't. I feel relieved to be with an equal.' And another man said: 'I have been married for sixteen years. My wife reaches orgasm only with some difficulty. I have been trying all means of helping her gain confidence and relaxation during intercourse, but I believe that there is a shade of jealousy in her mind about my easy satisfaction.'

All this could lead to feelings of guilt and negativity:

'I feel inadequate. Sometimes I wonder just how good a sex partner I am. But I guess we all have those doubts.'

'I feel I am at fault. It's something I have done wrong.'

'I have not done enough or the "right" thing.'

'I failed her.'

'I must be inadequate.'

Men's Feelings About Giving a Woman Clitoral Stimulation to Orgasm

In 1976, women's need for clitoral stimulation to orgasm, not coincidental to intercourse, became a public issue. For many men, this was the first time they encountered these facts. How did they react to this new information? What were men's general attitudes toward the clitoris? When men were asked 'How do you feel about the clitoris?' many answers included jokes or satirical remarks:

'How do I feel about the clitoris? I feel in awe of the little bugger. It's gotten so much publicity and become the focal point of so much rancour that I have the urge to salute it when I see it.'

'A woman's clitoris is the greatest thing since the mop – other questions redundant.'

In many other answers, the importance of the clitoris was brought into question by the frequent use of diminutives[5]:

'A woman's clitoris is a wonderful little thing.'

'The clitoris is a mysterious little "love button".'

'I think it is cute as it peeps out from its hiding place. Sometimes girls call it the "tickle button".'

'Big surprises come in little packages.'

'Cute little devil.'

But there were enthusiastic and positive remarks too:

'It is the primary erotic centre of her body, tender and sensitive, and has to be treated with great care and emotion.'

'It's just as important to her as my penis is to me.'

'Beautiful, stimulating, the most sensual part of a woman's body.'

'The clitoris is the blasting cap on a stick of dynamite. It is the trigger mechanism which puts everything else into motion.'

'It's the most important part of the vulva. A man that has loved a woman and cares for her knows these things.'

'It amazes me. It's the centre of my wife's entire sexual being. Every square micron must be packed with nerve endings because of her reaction when I touch it or even get near it.'

'Very beautiful and mysterious.'

A few men professed complete neutrality:

'What do I think about it? Nothing really.'

'I never really felt anything about it emotionally.'

'Nothing special.'

Others had had either no experience or bad experiences:

'She won't let me touch it.'

'My wife says my finger hurts it.'

'The clitoris is a strange thing to me. It protrudes.'

'If that is the point she wants stimulated, I will stimulate it. But I don't have any special feeling about it any more than I have any special feeling about any other body part that isn't in plain sight. It's like asking me how I feel about her liver.'

'I could never find my wife's. She doesn't seem to have one. I'm not sure what the clitoris is.'

'I have no feelings about it. She shouldn't have one.'

When men were asked what the clitoris looks like, there were a wide range of replies – many containing elements of discomfort and unfamiliarity, and even sometimes hostility, again often using diminutives:

'A small hooded pink bump that enlarges on arousal.'

'It looks like a tiny worm which needs sunlight…very pale.'

'It looks good and tasty.'

'When the hood is pulled back, it looks like a red pea coming out of its shell.'

'Like the tip of a male cat's penis. It looks like a funny little critter peeping out of its house.'

'A tiny titty jelly bean (I like the red ones).'

'Like a grapefruit seed in a translucent veil of tissue.'

'Small, round, pink and sensitive. A pearly little head. I have not seen it as illustrated in books.'

'Why, it looks like a clitoris, of course.'

But most men said they had never actually seen the clitoris:

'Never seen one in real life.'

'Only seen them in books.'

'I've never seen one because the lights are off or my eyes are closed.'

'I've seen diagrams and photos but not my partner's clitoris – she admonished me not to "play doctor". Instead we have operated by verbal feedback, i.e., "further up…a little to the right". This seems to work OK.'

'The clitoris swells and is easier to find as a woman becomes aroused. But I have never turned on the lights, sat back and examined one, so I am unclear about the exact description.'

'I was never told about the clitoris, nor about the shape of a woman's vulva (apart from there being a hole there). Nor did I hear where the urethra was. So I've had some difficulty in finding my way in on various occasions. I haven't seen it or examined it in detail but believe I know where it is. Just inside the top of the main slit. Incredibly high up in fact, right out of the region that I used to consider as cunt.'

'I know where it's supposed to be according to the books but she's apparently fully hooded and it is never exposed. At the slightest pressure it rolls sideways and gets lost again.'

'From texts I've tried to learn best how to stimulate it, especially with my tongue.' (Age thirty-eight.)

'I read in a book in college that the clitoris was anatomically synonymous with the glans penis. I got the impression that it was much more "like a penis" than it turned out to be. I thought it would be much bigger (longer) than it actually is.' (Age thirty-three.)

When asked where the clitoris is, many of the answers were rather vague. Although the most common answer was 'at the top of the vagina', it is unlikely that most men think the clitoris is inside the vagina; therefore, are these men using the word 'vagina' to mean 'vulva'?

Clearer descriptions included the following:

'It's near the top of the "crack".'

'It's higher up than one would think – and farther away from the vagina.'

'It's at the upper end of the outer lips, near the pelvic bone.'

'At the top (pubic bone) end of the vagina.'

'At the base of the mons, sandwiched between several folds of flesh.'

Also notable is the emotional reaction this question created in some men:

'I could give an average location in centimetres from the top of the vagina, etc., but there are many more questions I could better spend the time on.'

'I would rather show than tell.'

'In the illustration on page six of "Sex for Third Graders".'

'Sure ain't in her nose.'

Similarities Between Clitoral and Penile Anatomies

There is a widespread misunderstanding of women's sexual anatomy. What we usually think of as the 'clitoris' is simply the exterior part of a larger interior structure. The extent of this interior clitoral network is quite large – comparable to the size of the penis and testicles in men. Inside the penis there are two cavernous bulbs the length of the shaft that fill with blood and thus cause erection. These same two cavernous bulbs exist in the female; however, in the female they are separate, each extending on one side of the vulva, beginning at the pubic area (the exterior clitoris) and going back on either side of the vagina. During arousal they fill with blood and cause the entire area to swell: this is why a woman's vulva becomes swollen and puffy, pleasurably sensitive to the touch. When orgasm occurs, the blood is sent out of these structures in waves by muscle contractions. In other words, the clitoral system is similar in size to the penis, but the clitoral system is interior, while the penis is exterior. Both systems are the same in the early embryo.

If men could understand the similarities of their structures to those of women, they could understand clitoral stimulation much more easily. For example, most men need stimulation at the top of their penis for orgasm, even though they feel the orgasm basically at the base of the penis and inside their bodies: stimulation at

76

the sensitive tip and around the rim leads to sensations deeper inside the body. In the same way, stimulation of the exterior clitoral area causes sensations deeper in the body and vaginal area, culminating in orgasm.

How do you feel about stimulating a woman clitorally by hand?

'I hate to admit it, but my wife's way of having orgasm used to really irritate me in the beginning. She always clenches her legs together, sometimes even twists them together while I am supposed to rub her clitoris. After all I had heard about a woman spreading her legs meaning she wants you, I felt that this was a rejection, and really, that there was something "weird" about her. It took a couple of years before we could talk about this. In the beginning, I just did what I thought she wanted, but I really resented it, and gradually I began to do it less and less enthusiastically, I guess. Finally, we had a fight about it. She said she thought I resented her orgasms, and I said I thought she was being selfish when she had them. She didn't need me at all. I wasn't involved, I wasn't inside her, and I wasn't getting stimulated (although I have to admit that sometimes it was a pretty sexy situation, with her doing all that moaning and groaning, writhing and getting hot and sweaty, saying she loved me and grabbing me after – wow, very passionate kisses). Anyway, I still resented it. She was very hurt that I didn't enjoy her orgasms and didn't want to have sex for a while. That got me started thinking, what was the point of sex anyway? It's taken me a long time to begin to accept that this is how she (women?) has orgasm, and that it doesn't mean that there is anything wrong with me because she doesn't do it during intercourse. I mean, I know rationally that this is it, clitoral stimulation, and I really dig it, but at the same time, the myth of how it should be is still there.'

Most men who had tried it expressed doubts about their expertise at giving manual clitoral stimulation. When asked 'Do you feel knowledgeable and comfortable stimulating a woman clitorally? How do you feel while giving clitoral stimulation with your hand?' most mentioned feelings of discomfort and said that getting feedback from the woman was essential:

'I don't feel sublimely confident when dealing with a clitoris; the orgasm seems very picky about what it likes and what it doesn't like, and it's hard to know, until you get to know a girl pretty well, just what the right thing is.'

'Sometimes I can't find a woman's clitoris. I am either constantly getting lost – or the damn thing moves around a lot.'[6]

'I feel knowledgeable about touching a clitoris up to a point (get it?), and then I want her to communicate to me what she likes. I'm no mind-reader, and different women like different pressures and motions, although I find that they often are so glad to have their joy button get any attention at all that they go up the walls.'

'I don't think I'm doing it right. I've talked about it with the other guys, but all I hear are stories about "sticking your whole goddamn fist up there" while "she was getting wet to her ankles" crap.'

'It's exciting to stimulate a woman clitorally and see her sexual arousal. My girlfriend told me I was too rough sometimes. I was never too gentle, or then she didn't say anything.'

'Generally I feel knowledgeable about touching it, but some differ so radically in preferences that one can never be sure.'

'After ten years my wife finally conceded to letting me touch her but was very embarrassed in those days, but not today. I enjoy giving my wife stimulation, but I have to keep myself stimulated too with my other hand because she cannot hold my penis during her stimulation – it distracts her and she can't come.'

A few men said they felt they were doing something 'abnormal' that they should not need to do. A few connected manual clitoral stimulation with 'teenage' behaviour, calling it a high-school activity or adolescent behaviour, something they had done only before intercourse was possible. Still, in 1981, according to my data, most men had never given a woman an orgasm with manual clitoral stimulation!

When asked 'Do you get sexually excited by stimulating your partner? Do you enjoy her orgasm physically? Emotionally?' many men were very enthusiastic and commented on how much they enjoyed stimulating their partner to orgasm in this way. Some said it was great, even to stimulate her to multiple orgasms:

'How do I feel? Proud!'

'It's an ego trip.'

'I feel flattered.'

How do you feel about a woman stimulating herself?

But can a woman also stimulate herself manually while she is with a man? In the same way that men said that women often don't give them the correct manual stimulation of their penis, isn't it difficult for one person (especially of the opposite sex) to know just how to stimulate another? Although learning to do just that with a specific partner can be very loving and exciting, it is also very important for men and women to feel that they can stimulate themselves during sex with a partner. This can be an extremely intimate activity, while at the same time removing many frustrations and pressures from both the woman and the man.

How do you feel if a woman stimulates herself to orgasm with you? During intercourse?

Most men had never experienced a woman stimulating herself (manually) while close to them; for most men, having the woman give herself an orgasm was a new idea. As one man said: 'No woman has ever shown me how or even admitted to masturbation.' In fact, many men were shocked by the idea that their partner could masturbate to orgasm at all, even when alone; most men did not know how (or if) she did it. When asked 'Does your partner masturbate to orgasm? How? If you don't know, would you like her to share this information with you?' many gave answers similar to the following:

'No. I don't think so.'

'I don't think she ever has.'

'Don't know or care – probably on rare occasions.'

'She and I orgasm together if possible but I have a tough time holding mine.'

Many men did not like the idea of the woman stimulating herself while with them:

'It's OK if she has to, but I would feel let down that I can't please her.'

'I would feel inadequate if she did that.'

'There would be a tinge of personal failure.'

'I would resent it.'

'I hope it never happens. I would get up and leave.'

'I feel very uncomfortable when she masturbates while I watch. I feel left out, an audience, unimportant, merely an afterthought on her part.'

'It would be like I didn't satisfy her.'

'Why does she need me?'

And many had mixed feelings about it:

'It's not much fun being pushed out of the way, but I don't mind having expert guidance.'

'It wouldn't hurt my ego but it would disturb me if she climaxed that way only.'

'I feel strange – happy that she'll reach orgasm, but unhappy because I'm not doing it to her liking.'

'I don't feel too bad, as long as I'm the mental stimulation.'

'If I am feeling OK about myself, I feel OK when a woman reaches orgasm by stimulating herself on me. When I'm not feeling OK, I tend to feel used.'

And with a vibrator?
'I'd rather she came without a vibrator.'

'A vibrator is cancerous, probably.'

'Anything to make her come.'

'I feel no good if she needs a vibrator to orgasm.'

'Clitoral stimulation is OK but it's carrying it too far when she uses a vibrator!'

'I am very happy she does not use one.'

'Something about vibrators bothers me, but I don't complain to the one person I know who likes to incorporate one into the act.'

'If a woman stimulates herself to orgasm with me, I feel cheated. I would like to bring her to orgasm, and if I'm not, why am I her lover? Vibrators are for shit as far as I'm concerned.'

But other men expressed an open attitude toward trying one:

'I intend to buy a vibrator to see if we can enhance our sex life. I hear they're great.'

'I never experienced it, but I would enjoy watching her use a vibrator.'

'I would not mind my partner using a vibrator if I also took part, e.g., manipulating or helping manipulate the vibrator while kissing and fondling her breasts, etc.'

And a few men enjoyed the use of the vibrator by a woman:

'I love to watch her body spasmodically orgasm while she uses her vibrator.'

'My lover does not orgasm from intercourse – but we do many things together besides intercourse. It is very exciting to masturbate together. She has orgasms when she wants to – she just grabs the vibrator.'

'I really loved using the vibrator we had on my lover, as I could give her intense orgasms that way.'

'I am thrilled, frankly, that she is so into sex. She apologizes, and I have to keep encouraging her. The nitwit. It's like me eating a whole meal, and her feeling she must nibble.'

Cunnilingus

Although most men liked cunnilingus and were more familiar with it than manual stimulation, it was not a major way of giving women clitoral stimulation to orgasm. Only 32 per cent of the men who answered said that they usually continued cunnilingus until the woman reached orgasm. However, most men were extremely enthusiastic about cunnilingus. For just over half of the men who answered who enjoyed sex with women, cunnilingus was the second most popular sexual activity, after intercourse. But a large number of men felt squeamish about cunnilingus – including many of those who were enthusiastic about it. There were very few in-between opinions about cunnilingus, and the answers show a much greater emotional reaction than those to almost any other subject.

Although most men thought of cunnilingus as 'foreplay', they felt more comfortable with this form of clitoral stimulation than with manual clitoral stimulation. In fact, when asked about 'clitoral stimulation', most men began discussing oral sex, not mentioning manual stimulation unless it was specifically referred to by the question. Still, the form of cunnilingus practised by most men did not include much specific clitoral stimulation, but was more likely to concentrate on the general vulva and/or vaginal opening, rather than the clitoris. While this can be very pleasurable, both physically and emotionally, and even preferable to many women, lack of precise clitoral stimulation for orgasm is a drawback if no other provision is made for the woman's orgasm during sex.

Do you enjoy cunnilingus with a woman? What do you like and/or dislike about it?

Many men were extremely enthusiastic about cunnilingus:

'More than anything else I enjoy oral sex. If my partner wants, I will eat her all day long. I feel very happy, content, secure and loving doing so. I adore the texture, feel and taste, and also the lovely way a woman seems to respond while being eaten. The women I have had oral sex with seem to relax and very much enjoy being eaten. We both seem to have very good feelings about oral sex. There seems to be a very open feeling between us.'

'Oral sex with a woman is my favourite of all. I feel a great closeness, a deep intimacy burying my face in that dark secret place. I feel that she trusts me fully. I love to look up and see her eyes closed and her face contorted in exquisite agony. I love my face drenched in her secretions, and her clit dancing under my tongue and her rocking hard and arching her back. And especially her moaning, screaming, raising her arms above her head so I can see her armpits. I love the convulsive motions of her coming. I love it when it's over and I keep my face between her legs and it gets dry and sticky and our skin pulls when it peels apart.'

Others were ambivalent about the taste and smell:

'My wife repels me four out of five times. Sometimes her genitals smell like a chicken dinner.'

'First you sniff it, if you wouldn't lick it, don't lick it.'

'Some gals smell strong at first but if you just get going, it's like eating Limburger cheese. Smells rough but tastes great.'

'As the taste and smell are strong, I sometimes have to be slightly deliberate about first contact, but no more so than when eating, say, a particularly ripe cheese or unusual fruit, drink, spice, etc. – once you get a good sniff or taste, then whatever the initial apprehensions, it's enjoyable. And anyway, it's her.'

'Occasionally during a woman's cycle the smell is more of a turn-off than a turn-on initially. If I "kiss" her anyway the smell soon becomes a turn-on.'

Of course, yeast infections could disrupt the natural smell:

'Several minor vaginal infections, including trichomonas, produce an off odour. I'm confident that I can diagnose trichomonas by the odour-flavour.'

'Once in a while she's had some sort of vaginal infection that produces a strong and definitely unpleasant smell, an odour of old sweat and decaying fish.

I don't like it. She understands, but I've never found a way to tell her that without making her feel hurt. I wish I could say, "Hey, you've got that symptom again" without making it sound like a moral accusation.'

Some men hadn't decided yet:

'Female genitals are fragrant. Taste wonderful and my only complaint is a really, really raunchy crotch that hasn't been washed. But it's not really a true complaint since I've never experienced one – I just think that if someone didn't wash for two weeks it would smell foul.'

'What I dislike is that some women have an offensive – well, not really offensive but strange – smell. I'm still trying to get used to it.'

But some men had none of these negative associations:

'Many men and women find a woman's sex to be unclean in some way. I enjoy showing the woman that not only do I find her sex not unclean, but in fact I find it extremely delightful.'

'Would you believe that some women are reluctant to engage in such an activity since a lot of them have hang-ups and prehistoric beliefs that they smell bad? Usually my partner showers before the activity and it smells clean and tastes great with all the woman juices.'

'Many women have a tendency to push your face away from their genitals as though they feel they've done something wrong or smell bad. It is hard to convince them that I enjoy the smell and taste – and I do.'

'My wife cleans too much.'

'For me, cunnilingus is beautiful but only when the woman enjoys it. Some get pretty freaked out about it. The smell and taste is something exquisite. It can get a bit raunchy at times, but on the other hand, a freshly scrubbed cunt can be pretty tasteless and lose a lot of appeal.'

Some men emphasized that they liked the taste very much:

'Darndest thing: women taste so sweet down there. Without using anything added. Just reasonably clean. It's really nice.'

'Tastes and smells always excite me. Tastes vary – sometimes they are sweet and sometimes a little salty or tangy.'

'The taste is a very plain taste with just a slight distinctness which I like and which also arouses me.'

'Most are sweet and creamy.'

'I love the way my wife's genitals taste and smell, the way her pussy looks and feels, the heat and velvety wetness of it.'

'I like, in fact, just adore, the taste of women's genitals.'

In fact, of the men who mentioned feminine-hygiene sprays or flavoured creams, most said they did not like them: 'Women taste great (if clean and if they're not using any of those hygiene sprays). Their odour is a definite sexual turn-on and the taste is superb.'

'All the women I've gone with have been clean and washed. I like the natural woman taste and smell and do not like the use of the "vaginal mouthwash" sometimes advertised. All that advertising serves to separate people from each other, makes them think they stink and are ugly, and uses sexuality for profit.'

And other men emphasized that they liked the smells:

'The taste is faintly salty; there's a delicate smell that's very distinctive, but I can't describe it. I like it. Sometimes I've gotten it on my fingers and long afterwards I can hold them to my nose and still get a trace of that lovely scent.'

'Smells (the healthy ones) have become increasingly attractive to me with age.'

'The taste is good but not as exciting as the smell.'

Shere Hite

Are women's genitals 'clean'?

Although many men liked cunnilingus very much, almost half of those who answered were also preoccupied with whether the woman or the woman's genitals were 'clean':

'I'm learning more and more to enjoy cunnilingus. It's been hard to do – I have uncomfortable feelings about oozing: I was raised clean, clean, clean. I like to take a shower after sex.'

'If you want to have oral sex with a gal, I am saying to her, 'You are clean.'

'I'm still kind of squeamish about cunnilingus and still think of female genitalia as dirty. Most of my earliest sexual experiences were with women whose genitals were dirty and really did smell awful. I sometimes enjoy oral sex with women when I first establish that they're clean. I like the musky, sweet smell of a woman and get some pleasure from cunnilingus for myself, but mainly get into it to please the woman.'

'My partner usually washes just before or at least a few hours before and is either tasteless or pleasantly scented. Stale, unwashed female genitals taste and smell bad to me.'

'How does one ask a woman politely to wash?'

'Female cunt is not good-looking but I love it, every inch of it, if it is clean.'

'I like everything about oral sex with my lover-wife as long as she has secretly showered (I like my partners "clean") – taste, smell, texture, the pleasure it gives her, the turn-on to me.'

'I think women usually consider their pubic area "unclean, smelly, dirty, slimy, etc." Pardon me, but I would rather make that distinction. If I find a distasteful (no pun intended) situation, I'll suggest an erotic, arousing shower together.'

'I only like it after a bath. I don't like the taste of urine or stale secretions. Or the smell of faeces. But a clean pussy tastes good, believe me!'

One of men's most frequent 'buts' about the vagina and vulva is related to whether the woman is clean or has washed recently. While the fact that all bodies need bathing rather regularly would seem to go without saying, no men mentioned the necessity for brushing teeth regularly to make kissing pleasant. The fact that so many men saw fit to stress this point with regard to women's vulvas seems to reflect the influence of the age-old patriarchal view of female sexuality (and women) as being 'dirty', 'nasty' or 'not quite nice'. Each child still learns this in the story of Adam and Eve: it was Eve's sexuality and 'desire for carnal knowledge' which ruined the Garden of Eden and for which men and women are still being punished – especially women, who are told that they must henceforth bring forth children in pain and suffering. And of course women who are overtly sexual are often punished by society's double standard, which still categorizes them as either 'good women' or 'bad women'.

Unfortunately, for centuries in our society, women's sexuality has been considered 'dirty': a sensual, sexual woman is a 'tramp', 'dirty', 'filthy' and so on, whereas a sexual man is very masculine, admirable. The vulva, of which women are taught to be ashamed (the medical term for the vulva is '*pudendum*', a Latin word meaning 'of which one ought to be ashamed'), has been hidden away for so long that few people really know what it looks like. The general impression many men have is of a dark, wet place with an unfamiliar smell, a kind of unknown space into which the penis ventures courageously. One of the early triumphs of the women's movement was to reclaim the beauty, strength, and dignity of women's bodies for women, and to emphasize that it is women who own women's bodies, and not men. Women for the first time felt that they had the right to explore their own bodies and look inside them. With a mirror and a light and a plastic speculum a woman could see her interior, suddenly finding it to be a beautiful glossy pink, clean and dazzling – as opposed to the dark and unpleasant place she might have been led to believe she would find.

Perhaps men who still feel they are affected by these stereotypes about women's genitals can overcome them by also looking inside a vagina once, with someone they care about. Some men have seen their wife's or partner's vagina during a joint physical examination, conducted by a gynaecologist or sex therapist. This technique was originated by Drs Leon and Shirley Zussman, and has had excellent results.

A few men commented on cunnilingus during menstruation:

'I like the warmth and moisture of my partner's genitals, and I enjoy the very pleasant odour of them. The only time I do not like cunnilingus is during her period, although I have done it and was surprised that I could not tell the difference in taste or odour.'

'I love the smell of my lover's vagina while she is menstruating. I want her to menstruate in my mouth and on my face – it tastes so sexy and smells so good.'

'The smell and taste of a menstruating vagina does not appeal to me, though I have never tasted one.'

'Some women have a psychological hang-up of feeling dirty during this time. Why should they? Aren't they proud to have such sophisticated bodies? Aren't they proud that they are women?'

'As I grew up I was led to believe that this was the time of the month when a woman discharged all the poison and disease germs from her womb. I know better now, but still am hung up about it.'

'Menstruation makes little difference to me. Oral sex with a tampon in place is just the same as when she is not menstruating. Without a tampon, I reserve the right to refuse, but that is unlikely.'

'I feel more "afraid" of the vagina at that time. I'm less likely to play with it, to touch it or feel it. I rule out oral sex completely. She is hornier when menstruating. I will not hesitate to have intercourse.'

'I ate one girl who later said she was menstruating at the time, but I guess I was too wrapped up in it to care. Blood, blood, I had enough of it on me in Vietnam not to worry about it.'

How do women's genitals look?
Many men had ambivalent feelings about the looks of women's vulvas. On the other hand, some men liked them very much and offered beautiful descriptions. The range of answers covered every attitude imaginable:

'Better than men's.' 'Like "raw flesh" – a horrible mismatch.'

'I wish they were dry. Moisture bothers me. It looks like the skin of an old woman on a young one.'

'Gorgeous.'

'They look mysterious.'

'Inviting.'

'They look hairy, sensual, puffy, excited, red and full. A pretty furry pet animal.'

'Ugly but appealing and nice to touch.'

'Like a damp rose, petals blossoming.'

'Strange and compelling, inviting and ripe for explorations.'

Some men described why they liked its appearance:

'I love my wife's genitals. They look big, pink, wet, warm, ready for fun, ready to respond to me, mysterious, powerful, something to explore. Wow!'

'I think women's genitals are about as lovely as something on this earth can get. I love the way they taste and smell. There have been some genitals about which I held a near-religious feeling; this was because they were attached to women for whom I felt a deep love.'

'I think a woman's – my friend's when I peeled off her pants – genitalia are so beautifully shaped and designed! What was very nice was that her pubic hair was very blond and the moon shone in the window as I put my head between her legs.'

Men, Women and Vibrators

Should women use vibrators to reach orgasm when they are having sex with a man?
An increasing (and already large) number of women use a vibrator for orgasm when on their own or during masturbation. Incidentally, most women

who use vibrators for orgasm during masturbation do not penetrate themselves with the vibrator, even if they have one that is shaped like a 'dildo' or a penis – often they buy them since they are the kind most commercially available.

Even though an electric (battery-operated) massager is the easiest way for many women to reach orgasm, most women who normally masturbate using a vibrator do not try to use it during sex with a man. They fear his reaction: many of those who have tried to use one with a man say that most men resist incorporating a vibrator into sex with a woman, even if they accept the principle of clitoral stimulation to orgasm as necessary for women.

As one woman writes: 'I am thirty-three years old, living happily with Peter. He – the man I am living with for six years now – knows I use a vibrator when I masturbate (not the dildo kind you insert, just a small round neck-type massager that runs on a battery), but he never likes it when I try to use it in our lovemaking. I would love to use it because I think it's sexy and I can come very easily that way – I want to let myself go more with him, have orgasms while we are kissing and playing around and not worry about it. But if I pull it out, it seems to stop him. Now, sometimes I come to orgasm with him, but not always. Whether I have an orgasm seems to be an unspoken question between us, and this makes me feel tense sometimes, even if I come.

'I feel guilty saying this (is there something wrong with me?), but to really, really come to my heart's content (a lot), I have to have a serious session with my vibrator. Maybe he thinks I should "give up my dependency on the vibrator" – but I've tried, I guess I'm just not as secure while he uses his hand, I worry he will stop (just when I'm starting to come) and won't give me the continuous smooth stimulation I need (will he be bored? feel oppressed?) So I can't really let go and fantasize or focus on feeling that increasing glorious sensation when he is doing it…'

There is no reason why a man and woman today cannot use a vibrator as a regular part of lovemaking. Also, a vibrator is a good way to break through the shyness and newness that can accompany both people getting to know what it is like for the woman to have an orgasm, often several orgasms in a row. In this way, a man can observe a woman's timing and habits in the same way that women get to know the likes and dislikes of 'their man' during sex, how he reaches orgasm.

Any man who fears that a vibrator is 'unnatural' should ask himself if he listens to a radio, or drives a car, before criticizing women for using 'gizmos' and 'electronic devices'. Men, after all, are receiving a time-honoured form of adequate stimulation for their orgasm during coitus: therefore they do not need 'mechanical help'. This does not mean that they are biologically superior!

Some men see the vibrator as a pleasant enhancement of everything else that is going on. A vibrator of any size or shape can be held by the man and the woman together, or by either one of them. Most important: a man should not make a woman feel that she is alone while using it. For example, if a woman presses it to her mons/clitoral area or crotch, the man can put a finger in her vagina or caress her anus and kiss her, play with himself or 'talk dirty' to her. This is an activity for two, not one.

[1]   Most women masturbate to orgasm very regularly, especially when not reaching orgasm with a partner; just because women's desire for orgasm has often been hidden from society does not mean it is any less than men's.

[2]   This figure reflects the answers of 3,019 women in *The Hite Report on Female Sexuality*.

[3]   For a discussion of the differences between *The Hite Report on Female Sexuality* and Masters and Johnson's research on this issue, see *The Hite Report on Female Sexuality*, Chapter Three. Basically, Masters and Johnson have said that women should get sufficient indirect clitoral stimulation from the penis's traction on the skin surrounding the vagina, which is indirectly connected to the skin covering the clitoris, to reach orgasm. However, *The Hite Report on Female Sexuality*, based on a much larger sample, found that this was not effective in practice for the large majority of women, who need more direct clitoral stimulation for orgasm.

[4]   These statements are included here because, though they seem unremarkable, they were very rare.

[5]   The exterior clitoris as we know it is only a part of a very large internal clitoral network, which is as large as the penis.

[6]   Once again, these replies were much more likely to contain jokes than answers relating to intercourse or other topics.

Chapter Five

Sex And Violence: Part Of 'Men's Nature' Or Part Of The Culture?

Domestic Violence against Women: Why?

Women are facing an increasing climate of violence and sexual attack, statistics tell us. Although it is often said that 'women's new freedom and independence is causing the problem of domestic violence' this is not the heart of the matter. It is not women's 'independence' that causes a problem but an outdated mentality, glorified in films, novels and media, that defines maleness that is causing the problem (for both men and women) and needs to be updated. After all, to blame 'independence' would imply that women should end the violence by becoming docile wives and mothers 'again', not seeking 'independence' – yet certainly the West today stands for equal dignity and human rights for women and men.

While it is commonly implied that women's increasing independence is provoking men to this violence, this is unjust; society prefers to point the finger of blame at women rather than at the criminals or at an outdated ideology creating a certain formula of 'masculinity', praising male dominance, that boys and men learn. Not every man is a 'victim of male ideology', of course; many are independent thinkers who have innovated new, positive patterns of relating to women; unfortunately, others learned to take to heart militaristic slogans of what being 'a real man' means: i.e., 'a real man tells his woman what to do – just like his father.'

What about punishment for domestic violence as a solution? It did have a strong salutary effect in New York and elsewhere when batterers were arrested when police answered routine calls about domestic violence, shown on television handcuffed and being taken away by police – violence rates went down.

A long-term solution is to change the value system being absorbed by boys, i.e., cease the current glamorizing of military behaviour causing a rebirth of the idea that 'men should be tough', that same ideology that accepts bullies in schoolyards who prove that 'might is right' by picking on smaller boys or ridiculing boys who do not 'fight back' as 'men should' – otherwise labelling them as 'wimps who can't take it'. We can change the social messages to boys about what it means to be a man, offer better definitions.

An even deeper analysis may be this: the increase in violence to women also parallels the growth of the 'family values' movement. As it is being asserted that the increase in violence parallels the increase in women's independence, the question is: why is that connection more logical than connecting the growth of violence with other trends in society? Immediately I would like to say that the alternative to family values society is not a pornographic society! I am not against 'family values' *per se*, but 'family values' traditionally interpreted as meaning the father as the owner of the family and the woman as servant. What I mean by 'family values' is a loving group in which both male and female contribute as much as they can to each other, giving love and support.

Family values pressures, as defined in the old sense, may be causing some of the pressure and violence. For example, it may be the very pressure on women and men to 'get into the right kind of marriage and be satisfied' – form a 'perfect traditional family' – that is contributing to this violence. Many men are faced with a new domestic situation and feel that the behaviour they will be approved of for using to handle this 'rebellion' is force or even violence – or they do not know any other way to deal with their emotions in the face of the situation. Indeed the violence is not so much a result of the increasing independence of women as it is a result of the current climate of social pressure insisting that women be 'good wives and mothers' who 'accept everything', and pressure insisting that men 'take care of them all' and 'be dominant' – so that if the family is dysfunctional, if neither role fits, violence is the result. This of course does not mean that we should condone such violent behaviour!

'Family values' proponents often turn a blind eye to the fact that the family has always contained domestic violence and that divorce was common in previous centuries. Over the last hundred years such advocates have become increasingly moralistic about 'the family', pressuring women and men to fit into it more than they were pressured in the nineteenth century when fewer marriages took place. There were no statistics on domestic violence kept during the 1950s, the heyday of the family, while the family began to fall apart in the 1960s. This was not because of women's independence – men declared their independence of the family in the 1960s, and the Women's Movement only started after that, between 1968 and 1969 – but because the institution itself did not function properly.

In short, one could say that the self-righteous moralism of those who push 'family values' is causing this violence to increase and that women are once again paying the price of submission. It is just as logical to say this as to assert a knee-jerk response implying that women are being 'bad' and 'rebellious' and thus themselves causing the violence.

Blaming women themselves for the violence done to them ('they are too independent') is similar to the old mentality that used to judge women in rape trials: it was said that a woman was guilty herself or had caused the rape if she had been wearing a short skirt, bright lipstick or displaying any sign that she wished to be sexually attractive, or if it could be shown that she had had unmarried sex with other men – rather than focusing 'the problem' on the rapist himself. The unwritten law asserted that men were not responsible, since 'they are male animals who cannot help it, they need to do it'; thus the ideology gave them carte blanche. Today we see things differently.

Women's increasing autonomy and belief in themselves – not basically about the right to wear short skirts, no matter what some media imply – is energizing and benefiting society including each and every one of us, women, men and children, and must be encouraged! Not to do this is to remove a great energy from our society.

The argument that women who are 'rebellious' cause needless problems, that they should happily accept the role offered to them as mothers, is also heard in Middle Eastern politics, but such points of view are not realistic and do not include the view that women have as much right to self-determination as men do.

Another argument often heard is that violence against women is increasing because of the current climate of 'sexual openness' and 'women's freedom' that has come about during the last twenty-five years. It is said: if women today want to 'go out and be free, sexually curious', they deserve to be punished: like modern embodiments of Eve, these 'devil women' need to be saved from themselves. It is also asserted that sex and violence are innately connected, that 'what else can you expect when you don't impose a moral order on men's inevitable desires'?

In order to hide views 'justifying' violence to women, some critics lump together 'female freedom', 'women's rights', pornography, miniskirts, consumerism, rock music and drugs, often blaming 'the new free woman' for them or using them as symbols of 'the problem'. Islamic Fundamentalists sometimes use images of Western 'free women' in miniskirts to illustrate this attitude.

The litany against consumerism and drugs appeals to people who feel a deep disquiet and alienation facing a changing family dynamic; people may also be susceptible to these irrational arguments because they feel unhappy in today's cold market values society which seems to demand that the individual be productive or else irrelevant.

Many people today believe that the West has become corrupt, that women are 'too free', too money-oriented, that sex is 'too easy', that now women should 'go back into the home where they belong', stop having these independent ideas, things were better before. Things were simpler, according to such beliefs – but were they? Society has always looked for such easy explanations, especially when it has not understood the process of cultural change.

We are in the midst of a very profound period of change. The demand for women's equality and equal human rights with men has profound implications – in the areas of work, equal pay and advancement, access to top positions, personal life and sexuality.

The legitimate desires of women and girls, men and boys, to create a new society in which women are equally valued with men are sometimes falsely linked to 'the new world of pornography and cheap sex'. You often hear it said: 'Women today don't know anymore how to take care of the family, or what real love is. They have lost their beauty, they just want quick sex, sex, sex! How superficial they are…'

To link women's new rights and autonomy with current market values or a superficial view of female sexuality is incorrect and insulting to women. Pornography, for example, does not represent 'women's freedom'; most pornography is owned and directed by men and in fact depicts old values in which women are either 'sexy devil-temptresses' or 'good mothers at home'. It reasserts the 'devilish' view of female sexuality, which has hurt both women and men so much in the past. Pornography seeks, under the guise of being about 'the new sexual freedom', to subjugate women even more than before while justifying men's violence to women: 'he's lustful and gets carried away like all male animals, he can't help himself.'

Women did not create 'the sexual revolution' or the current pornographization of so many parts of society, from art to advertising. To blame their 'independence' is illogical. Rather, women have been agitating for their rights in general, not demanding pornography or 'sexual freedom'; in fact, they demanded sexual equality, which is a different matter, one that is still being worked out. To be clear: the Women's Movement holds that women have the right to choose to be married or 'single', to have children or not have children, and so on. Yet the old moral system holds that every woman who is not married by the time she is thirty must be 'one of those women', that a woman who is not married after her early twenties and has a sex life is probably a 'slut' or worse... The Women's Movement has shown that this is part of an old system of values oppressing women and their calls for change. This began at the same time during the 1970s when a differently oriented movement for 'sexual freedom' was making newspaper headlines; thus the two movements (related but different) were merged by the media, creating this confusion that remains with us today. Thus to blame the Women's Movement for what is causing the violence to women seems irrational and to verge on the worst kind of scapegoating of women. The lurid pornographic styles so dominant in media and art now are signs of the end of the previous moral order, not a new 'amoral order'.

The movement to change society to include women as having equal rights with men in every area sees the future as enormously positive, based on an either male or female-headed household and a new, evolving way of relating inside a democratized family and at work.

The solution is not for women to become more docile and obedient; the Jews tried this in Germany before they were exterminated, thinking that surely if they would show that they were 'fitting in', they would be accepted, but they were not – they were killed. Rather, the solution is for the 'family values' and 'traditional family' propaganda to be lifted. In these days of 'fundamentalist revival', both West and East, there is increasing pressure on women to 'return to the family', to 'give up careers' and 'independence and all that', who say that 'motherhood is better' (even though in recent Spanish statistics, quite a few parents are murdered by their children); there is increasing pressure on men to 'be a man' in the military style: that is, to show dominance.

If some men's anger about change is coming to the fore, shouldn't there be a public debate about the traditional male value system? If it is based on a desire for domination, shouldn't new types of values and identities be shown, other types of male heroes?

While it is understandable that in some moments we all feel uncertain and insecure about the changes taking place – will society become more pornographic: i.e., value others only for their sexual prowess? Will we all act like 'animals' and stop having long-term relationships? Where are we going with these changes, what is the future? These fears are misguided, because we have a great opportunity.

We are in the middle of a change that is unprecedented in the last centuries of our history: remaking the social order in a way that gives women equal status with men, reinventing sexual culture, work culture and family culture – enormous tasks. Today's subtle changes in millions of individuals are aiming toward a new social order, one filled with more love, warmth and caring than we know at present, yet no longer based on the antiquated family system with its hegemony requiring that women submit to male authority or that men feel they are 'in charge' and 'responsible' for everyone, not able to interact equally with the others but required to act 'better than the others, and prove it'. A democratization of private life. For the better.

What we can all learn here is that each individual is worth a lot, the value of being who they are: men do not need to dominate women to have value, nor do women need to be in a traditional family or have children to have worth.

The Image of Men in Pornography: A Reality Check

Does the image of men we commonly see in pornography reflect who men really are sexually? It seems to me that pornography presents a highly distorted image of men. I don't believe that men are the monolithic beings depicted in most porno images, nor that they find their authentic selves in pornography. My research with thousands of men shows a different picture of who men are sexually whereas pornography represents the imposition of a rigid ideological view on male sexual feelings, expression and behaviour rather than a realistic depiction of male sexuality.

Ironically, while on the surface pornography seems friendly to men – more than to women – its underlying message makes fun of men. Subliminally it implies to men that their sexual expression is ridiculous, base, crude or insensitive, even grotesque. Visually it frequently makes men look ugly and coarse, foolish and unappealing. Who hasn't seen these porno images? They're all around us: in sex magazines, e-mail Spam on the Internet and even in 'fine art'. The makers and distributors of the images must believe men like them, that they are generally making 'what men like', because they market it to men, and the industry is growing. Although few women buy porno, industry spokespersons frequently claim that 'the number of women is increasing', any gain they refer to is fractional.

Do most men really like pornography? Do they identify with the images, or find them laughable, 'not really me' or do they think to themselves: 'I wish I could be like him, lucky guy?' Whether men like the way they are portrayed in porno is difficult to know, since most are brought up with the idea that if you find something revolting, you must not flinch but look it straight in the eye and say: 'Wow! I like it! I'm bad!' Boys are not supposed to shy away from 'vulgar things': doing that makes you 'girlish'. Therefore, the more disgusting a pornographic visual is, the more a 'real man' shouldn't show disgust. But, privately, do most men really think they are 'like that' – or do they experience their sexuality as more subtle, more diverse, possibly more erotic and even spiritual?

Of course not all men look at porno, so why is it generally considered for men? Is it because women supposedly don't need to jerk off? Or because the material puts 'men on top' as 'the winners', denigrating women as 'the losers'? In porno, there is a subliminal text in addition to the actual visual depiction. Men are almost always presented as predators with erections, almost as rapists; one of the key unspoken clichés of porno is that the man must show no feelings, no sentimentality, he must follow a strictly physical sexual scenario. Porno portrays men having pleasure focused on erection and ejaculation, rarely seeking eroticism for its own sake or other purely sensual activity, but never 'in love' or sexually active in a non-focused way. They do not show men seeking full-length body contact or needing to hold another person and be held, or to be penetrated themselves in some way. Sexual exuberance, desire, elation, love not satisfied by orgasm, fantasy: these states are about something other than a biological drive to reproduce the species, the 'male sex drive' that in pornography is central to 'sex'.

Today, 'male sex drive' as a concept has taken on a sort of mystical ring. During the late twentieth century this term was used more and more often, so that it became 'unquestionable truth' and today is assumed to be biological. But is it? Logically, if men supposedly have a biological drive to 'thrust', then shouldn't women have a complementary reverse 'drive' to open? Or, is the entire idea of 'sex drive' a fraudulent ideological category masquerading as scientific fact?

What about the other sexual states that men experience which are not seen in porno? Are men as singularly mechanical and aggressive 'by nature' as they are depicted? Society has tried to insist that a real man should 'get hard' at will, whenever appropriate, meaning in a private situation with a reproductively-aged female, but it is impossible to will an erection into being. In truth, the penis is a delicate part of the male being: one that responds with exquisite sensitivity to every nuance of emotion a man can feel. Erections come and go in men, during sex and during sleep. Most men report that it is desire they seek, not the mechanical means of orgasm or creating erection. Desire and arousal are the pleasures that spread through the body; orgasm, after all, can be attained alone during masturbation.

The beauty of male sexuality is not so much about erection as all the gestures and subtle meaningful body movements, including the ups and downs of erection – tumescence and non-tumescence, de-tumescence and re-tumescence – ways in which the body makes itself known or speaks. These movements represent a man's beauty and personality and are very erotic. Pornography as we know it does not represent that variety and diversity of expression, it simply pretends to be 'revolutionary' and 'avant-garde' by being 'shocking', passing itself off as 'incredibly open' when compared to the old value system. But it is not 'revolutionary'. Such images do not address a more valuable and interesting view of 'who men are sexually'.

What is 'male sexuality'? Why is it so closely identified with intercourse in a reproductive scenario? The answer involves understanding centuries of enforcement of the idea of 'sex' as an animalistic physical desire, to be controlled by putting it into a reproductive context within marriage. Yet this early ideology contained the seeds of its own destruction by furthering the idea that men are somehow in the harness of 'reproduction within marriage', that their sexuality can only be freely experienced outside the family. In my research, it seems that the ideological split between 'body' and 'mind' or 'soul' – as pornography depicts – is the crux of the problem men experience, not whether or not they are in a 'reproductive relationship'. The definition of sex created to go with our social order and family structure, originating about

3,000 years ago, has been focused on the reproductive act, to the detriment of other activities, because we have evolved from a culture that wanted to increase reproduction to one in which, now, most of us use birth control.

Men's 'sexual nature' is very 'polymorphous perverse', as the *New York Times Book Review* characterized the picture of men that emerges from *The Hite Report on Male Sexuality*. Men in my research show a great diversity as this extract shows: 'Masturbation: this can be one time a man expresses his sexuality without a focus on reproduction or coitus.' As one man puts it, 'I have more or less two sex lives, one with my wife and one with myself.' Men in my research say they enjoy masturbation or having sex alone because they can fantasize about whatever they want and there is no pressure on them to perform for another person. During masturbation, in my research, men stimulate themselves in many more places than they do when with a partner. And this one: Anal stimulation: in my research, men express a hidden desire to be caressed and 'penetrated' – possibly by a finger – anally, since just inside the anus in men (but not in women) there is proximity to a gland that when stimulated causes orgasm, so much so that most urologists stimulate men to ejaculation during their examinations in this way.

However, most men do not allow themselves to explore the various feelings they wish to express during sex with a partner, especially a female partner, but instead try to follow as 'perfectly' as possible the reproductive scenario depicted in most pornography. Our sexual acts have been channelled into too limited a form of expression; sex could be more interesting if it was not always focused on one scenario: foreplay followed by penetration, the high point being 'fucking' or coitus.

The appearance of Viagra and the fear of HIV have increased rather than decreased the focus on erection; for example, many men are nervous about having to put on a condom and consequently losing their erection or their sexual desire. Not only are men asked to use condoms, they are expected to provide clitoral stimulation to orgasm in many cases. But many men cut short foreplay because they are afraid they may lose the erection which they have been taught is necessary to enjoy sex and which would be 'shameful' to lose. More men could reach much higher peaks of feeling and arousal if they did not feel anxious about how they 'should' behave sexually.

Today, many men seem to be withdrawing from 'sex' in various ways. This withdrawal can take the form of claiming 'erectile dysfunction', 'religious purity' deferring 'commitment' or preferring non-standard, 'kinky' sex. This may be a reaction to the clichés that surround society's view of men, seen increasingly through modern advertising as well as pornography. If men are told they are 'cheap', their bodies mechanically obedient to 'lurid' stimulus (akin to the response of Pavlov's dogs to a dinner bell), of course the more sensitive men will react by withdrawing. It would be better to change outdated stereotypes of 'sex' than to withdraw, thus bolstering the ancient dichotomies that have caused a problem.

How do men feel about how they are depicted as treating women in pornography and about the violence to women shown in most pornography? Most men feel perplexed, and wonder why this can excite them. Although pornography frequently denigrates women – showing women beaten black and blue and liking it – it also denigrates men, cheapening and brutalizing their sensibilities, destroying the opportunity for personal sexual discovery, implanting clichés such as 'a real man is the one with the biggest, hardest erection', blocking their power to express themselves with others. In my interpretation, sex and violence are mixed during the Oedipal stage of boys' development, at the time when they are emotionally leaving the mother and simultaneously becoming increasingly sexual. But pornography's frequent implication that men are beasts whose underlying unchangeable natures make them likely to be violent to women is incorrect, misleading and dangerous.

Porno's messages bisect men psychologically, showing sexuality as separate from emotion and the soul. This can affect men in a very negative way, although many remain unconscious of the origin of their discomfort; these non-verbal messages cause them to think that they are 'two people' – the sexual 'animal' and the thinking, spiritual individual. One thinks of the separation of women and men in Moslem mosques. For this reason, the vast majority of men find it confusing when they actually fall in love, and mix body with soul. The increasing male aversion to falling into these stereotypes of male sexuality can also be seen in a broader political sense: male Islamic extremists in Afghanistan proclaimed in many of their public statements that they wanted to 'create a more pure society' that would be less sexual, a society in which women's bodies would be covered, hidden from sight – or were women being punished? Both Western and Eastern traditions pose a problem for men in terms of integrating 'mind', 'body' and relationships with women.

Pornography is above all propaganda – an ideological construct used to direct men toward a certain style of reproductive sexual activity, to tell them the kind of attitude they should have towards sex and women. Women in pornography serve the basic purpose of legitimizing the male sexual expression. Pretending to represent 'nature', pornography touts an ideological view of how men should behave. It is a brainwashing device. In fact, pornography is one of the areas of 'globalization' that presents the most negative outdated versions of who men are to the rest of the world; if we change our basic views of what sex is, then we will contribute to a better form of globalization.

Is Sexual Violence Part of Human Nature?

Fantasies of both women and men contain themes of violence and power. What does this mean? Is violence part of human nature (and therefore human sexual nature)? It is sometimes implied that the end product of sexual feeling is violence: that, if you let sex get out of hand or go too far, become bestial or instinctive, it will lead to violence? There is a belief that sex in its 'uncontrolled, natural state' leads to violence: that the individual has to control sex because in the end, it will lead to something negative and disastrous, like death. Of course, this is only true for those who have this wish in the first place: sexual feelings do not 'naturally' lead to death or destruction, even though they may be frenzied. To remind readers of the obvious: most of these beliefs come supposedly from Biblical tradition. For centuries various Biblical scholars or commentators argued that sexual women were 'tools of the devil', 'sexual temptresses' who could cause a man to go to his death if their 'siren song' was heeded. Centuries of rabbinical and Islamic commentators wrote interpretations of Old Testament and Talmudic scriptures 'proving' that this was their meaning, just as today Islamic groups like the Taliban follow certain clerics who wrote texts exaggerating specific points of Islamic scripture, insisting their interpretation was 'the one true way'.

Of course, such an ideological assertion that sex leads to violence means that logically sex has to be controlled by a series of moral imperatives, especially that women have to be controlled: a convenient conclusion for a society of patrimony and male dominance. This scenario, in which men are presented as naturally violent, is seen in much pornography. A typical pornographic scenario implies that inside every man there is a lurking stranger, a beast who wants to rape and pillage, that this beast exists inside men – but not women, since female 'human nature' is different. Robert L. Stevenson's *Dr. Jekyll and Mr. Hyde* is the classic depiction of the man with these two sides;

this nineteenth-century novel was made into several films, one with Spencer Tracy playing the serial killer who is a respectable doctor by day. A self-justifying but also self-wounding view, this is a clear depiction of the trap men are caught in by a culture that defines 'male sexuality' as not fitting into the system of the traditional family. Pornography reinforces the notion that, 'well, you have to let men have their way', 'boys will boys'; as it is also commonly said: 'men can't help it, you have to go along with them.' In other words, whatever a man wants, one has to placate him: one shouldn't challenge a man directly because that may arouse the sleeping beast, who could be violent...

Of course this is ideology, projecting a male 'nature' that is fantasy, not fact. Men are not innately violent, they are taught to be this way by 'sissy-bating' puberty rituals and an old cult of masculinity. However, society has invested in this view in part because by this means it believes it has channelled men's basic sexual expression into reproductive activity and allowed men an outlet for their anger over their restricted role, if they direct their anger at women.

The truth is that the penis is a delicate part of the male being, one that responds with exquisite sensitivity to every nuance of emotion a man can feel. Although the society has tried to insist that 'a real man' should 'act macho' and 'get hard' at will, many men do not find it 'natural' to 'act macho' (most men in my research do not feel excited by becoming violent), and as every man knows it is impossible to will an erection into being. The understanding of male sexuality needs drastic revision.

What about the violence women are said to have as 'dominatrices' and in their fantasies? After all, it is true that many women find fantasies of being raped and 'taken by force' exciting during masturbation and orgasm. First, to set the record straight, there are as many outrageously dishonest clichés running around about women as there are about men. One repeated subtext is that women like to be degraded sexually, that women like violence done to them in the end. This is to confuse violence and passion. On the other hand, pornography does contain many depictions of men being violent to women, or depictions of women tied up, bound and gagged (as part of sex); and even if this may excite some viewers, this does not prove that 'this is real human nature'. More likely, it proves that we have been conditioned to find this exciting and that the power relationships involved are exciting to us, not the violence.

As proof that women do not like to see themselves in these ways, do not agree that 'receiving violence' represents 'their sexual nature', sales of pornography to women have only increased in the most minuscule way over the last three decades – even though a greater increase was repeatedly predicted.

Clearly men do fall in love with women, despite cultural signals not to get 'too close' to girls, to 'stick with the boys', 'don't trust women', and so on. The question is: what do they do in reaction to the confused mixture of feelings this can arouse? Pressure on boys to express disdain and contempt for their mothers at the same time that there is pressure to begin to be 'sexual' toward women: these messages together become entwined and cause a traffic jam in boys' minds, sometimes short-circuiting their brains, fusing the two together forever It is not necessary for the culture to break men's spirit and enjoyment of love and passion in this way; it doesn't have to brutalize boys by taunting them with being 'momma's boys' if they refuse to categorize 'male' and 'female' so emphatically (and take a dominant posture as 'male') or if they refuse to ostentatiously join 'the male group' or stop being close to their mothers and sisters. After all, this socially-created 'male' way of thinking leads to the 'conquer all' mindset towards nature, love, work, other countries and races: changing it would have a positive effect internationally.

No one needs to blame themselves for becoming aroused by looking at images combining sex and violence, or for having 'rape fantasies' – male or female. Since we are all products of the culture; how could it be otherwise? But we should blame ourselves if we do not make any effort to change our way of thinking and being sexual.

Sexual Violence in the Culture

Where do pressuring women into sex, rape of various kinds, paying women for sex – either outright, or as many men said, in marriage or on dates – and buying women in pornography fit into men's lives – if at all? Are they things only 'abnormal' men are involved with, or did they in some way involve and affect all men's lives and relationships with women, because they somehow involve the basic underpinnings of the entire social structure?

If sexual intercourse has traditionally been the basic symbol of male domination and ownership of women, whether or not an individual man may feel this at any given time, then rape and paying women for sex or buying women through pornography are basic extensions of this ideology – not biologic 'urges' or part of a physical male 'sex drive'. It is what sex means to men that makes them sometimes want to rape or buy women, not a desire for orgasm or sexual sharing.

The general culture – in movies, books, jokes and popular sayings – reinforces the idea that men 'get' or 'take' sex from women, men 'have' women, men conquer and possess women, women say 'no' but mean 'yes', women 'give in' to men – and 'penetration' is the symbol of this victory. Men, brought up to feel that a vital part of being a male is to orgasm in a vagina, often resent women's 'power' to withhold this 'male need' from them – not realizing that this is in many ways the only 'power' left to many women. It is this dynamic that in part sometimes leads men to say that women are 'more powerful' than men.

In fact, the model of sex as we know it has even been called the 'rape model' of sex. If men have more power, money and privilege than women, can the definition of 'sex' change? Won't forcing women into sexual intercourse, either physically through rape, or financially through paying a woman or buying pornography, continue its appeal? Arguably a real and profound change may occur. Right now, in many ways 'fucking' and physical rape stand as an overwhelming metaphor for the rape – physical, emotional, and spiritual – of an entire gender by our culture.

Rape

Do men 'naturally' want to rape women?

'Sometimes I've found myself getting excited watching a show in which a man is planning a rape. It bothered me that I was being aroused by it. I'm not sure I understand why.'

'I have often wanted to rape a woman, and I fantasize about it a lot. But the idea disturbs me because it runs counter to my sense of mutual respect, humanism, feminism, etc. I'm really anxious to see what other men feel about rape.'

What does the physical rape of a woman mean to men? Is the desire sexual? A form of hostility and anger? Or a way to reassert an injured 'masculine pride'?

Many men think of rape as a way of putting a woman 'back in her place' – this was a man's right. Others say women are 'asking for it', the implication being that women have no right to be sexual unless it leads to intercourse with men and that men have the right to control women's sexuality:

'I've seen a lot of women who seem to be asking for it…just as a person with a fistful of money is asking for robbery by flaunting his money, especially in a gin mill or dark alley. I also feel sympathy for women. After all, when someone wants to protect one's money from being stolen, the money can be placed in a bank. But how does a woman protect her body from being raped? I wish I knew. A little more prudence, I guess. I'm glad I'm a man.'

'There is the provocation of "dry hustling". Dry hustling is making oneself available for sex and then withdrawing or withholding it. The brassiere-less woman in a public place is a dry hustler. The bra-less look is attractive. It is supposed to be. And it is a provocation.'

A few say rape is justified by the male 'sex drive' and the 'failure' of women to meet that 'need'. Underlying this point of view is the idea, strong in our culture and in all patriarchal cultures, that men own women's bodies. As one man said, 'She is mine. I have a right to orgasm through intercourse. God gave me the right when he made women for men.' A man should not have to masturbate for orgasm when sexual desire is not mutual, according to this point of view; he should have his orgasm through a woman at all times (only an orgasm had through intercourse with a woman is legitimate), and it is a woman's duty at all times to help him do this.

Also implicit in many of the replies is the idea that a woman denying a man sex is somehow denying his manhood and that by raping a woman a man is reasserting his masculinity – not only with the woman but also in his own mind:

'Once I was going with a woman (in high school) and she would not let me have sex. All my friends had done it with their girlfriends, and even did it with us when we went out on double dates and parked together after. I got to feel like a real reject. I could have lied to them about it, but then my girlfriend would have found out, and they probably wouldn't have believed me anyway, since I couldn't have described the feeling. This made me so angry I felt like raping her. Finally, without anybody knowing, I picked up a streetwalker and had intercourse. This did a lot for my feeling of confidence in my own masculinity. Soon after, I broke up with my girlfriend and started going with somebody else who would go all the way. Then I could tell the guys, and I felt like one of the group again.'

One man writes about his desire to rape being connected to the teachings of the culture:

'It's pretty obvious that I have some hostility toward women that started way back – they have something I want, and I'm a "bad boy" for wanting it – they're excluding me – they have a secret – they have a sex organ, but dirty little boys don't get any, etc., etc., ad nauseam. I have become aware of these feelings and know when they are active; when I feel them, I back off whatever situation is causing them and find something else to do.'

Another man describes chillingly his generalized feeling of rejection – feeling left out of what 'everyone else' is enjoying, what other men are having:

'I have certainly wanted to. Usually this desire comes after I have been rejected by a very attractive woman, e.g., at the office. Then I fantasize following her, putting a gun to her head (I own a revolver) and asking her something like "Now tell me who you want to go to bed with." In recent months, I have become more sympathetic toward rapists, because I see in myself the other side of the sexual revolution: it is all well and good for the Beautiful People to decide to bring their fantasies out of the closet and talk about the joys of sex in public – it is another to be tantalized day after day by the sight of beautiful women you desire but can't have. Apparently every one of them is experiencing the wildest sexual pleasures and fulfilment, because the media are everywhere saying so.'

The image of a rapist appeals to some men, who identify it with being strong and virile, passionate and powerful:

'I don't think I could. But I have been sort of impressed by people who pulled off what seemed to be an especially brilliant or daring rape.'

'I have fantasies of doing it, as a form of "proving" to the woman that I am really all "man", able to get and keep a hard-on and use it to force myself on her, whether she wants me or not.'

Some men even write that all 'real' men have a desire to rape women because this is part of a male's innate makeup (a 'natural' animal instinct[1]):

'Why do I want to rape women? Because I am basically, as a male, a predator and all women look to men like prey. I fantasize about the expression on a woman's face when I "capture" her and she realizes she cannot escape. It's like I won, I own her.'

'Rape behaviour in males today probably exists because it has been selected for (this would take precedence over selection by females) in the Darwinian model of natural selection[2]; as much as our contemporary society despises the rapist, we must admit that in man's history the rapist's genes were naturally selected because the behaviour had survival value.'

A few men wonder why they don't have these feelings, and if they are 'abnormal':

'I have never raped a woman or wanted to. In this I guess I am somewhat odd. Most of my friends talk about rape a lot and fantasize about it. The whole idea leaves me cold.'

In fact, despite the seeming secret admiration of some men for rapists as the ultimate 'man', strong and powerful, the reality is usually just the opposite: it is the man with the lowest self-esteem who is most likely to rape women or pressure them for sex – the man who does not see himself as strong and powerful, the man who feels the most rejected, the most like a 'loser'.

The loner-rapist who becomes violent is becoming more and more a common figure in our society – unfortunately:

'I am single, never married, never lived with a woman, and I am so alone that I am slowly going crazy. I am fifty pounds overweight, work as a clerk in a welfare office and as a security guard at nights. I find going out to meet women very frustrating. Going to dances and no one wanting to dance with me gets me pissed. I get very depressed and antisocial. I have a perverse but vicarious thrill in other people (usually men) who go berserk in public places and kill innocent bystanders, such as David Berkowitz (Son of Sam). When I was in college, I wanted to shoot good-looking co-eds on campus with a concealed automatic pistol. They never look at me or acknowledge my humanity, so maybe I'm not good enough for them. I think they're afraid I'm going to rape them. I would never rape a woman because I don't think I could convince them I'm serious, they'd probably scream and I would run. Berkowitz's strategy was more direct, hostile, vengeful, and upfront. I admire Berkowitz, Son of Sam, for what he did.'

Pornography and the Definition of 'Male Sexuality'

What is the reason for pornography's increasing importance in our society? According to *Forbes* magazine, by 1978, sex was a larger business than the record and film industries combined, amounting to $4 billion a year. Why do some men (and some women) use and look at pornography? Is it for sexual stimulation or 'male bonding' and identification? What 'turns men on' about pornography? Is it because of the viewing of female nudity or sexual activities? Or because of the fantasies of male power that accompany the viewing?

Certainly we all – men and women – have a right to see and read about intimate relationships between people – and in this way, to make more sense of our own lives and feelings. But pornography as we know it does not for the most part serve this purpose. In fact, much of pornography shows a woman submitting to a stronger, threatening, perhaps hostile and violent male.[3] Even in 'soft-core' pornography, in which a woman is alone on the page, perhaps making eye contact with the viewer but almost always in a 'come and get me' pose, the woman is being dominated too – not by a man in the picture, but directly by the viewer, who can use her in any way he pleases. Pornography as we know it – as, indeed, sex itself – is a reflection of the society, with women often being used for men's pleasure. The fact that men dominate women in most of these pictures is such a commonplace that it is not seen as remarkable.

Pornography also reinforces in men the idea that all women can be bought; as one man said: 'Pornography is a cheap way of buying a woman.' Pornography does not glorify women; most men have contempt for the women they see on the pages, no matter how beautiful. A common form of using pornography is for men to look at it together in a group and to make comments about the women. This is a form of male bonding and reinforces the idea of male ownership of women.[4] Pornography reminds one of slave markets and slave auctions: each man can appraise, select and buy the body that suits him. House slaves are the younger, 'prettier' women, while field slaves are the hard workers – domestics or wives. The economic pressures on women, especially poor women, to sell their bodies in this way are great.

The continued spread of pornography will make relationships between men and women much slower to change, because pornography reinforces in men so many of the old and stereotyped attitudes to women and toward themselves that have done so much damage – both to women and men – already. This is true just as much of pornography that shows women dominating men as it is of depictions of men dominating women, since this is only a role reversal and still centres on the same definitions of sex involving all the issues we have discussed in this book so far. Pornography keeps men believing women are the way they want women to be, or have been told women are (either submissive or dominant, 'bitchy') and fortifies men's belief in their own sex role. Men, reading and looking at pornography, know they are sharing in something other men see and assume therefore that this is what all 'real men' want, identify with, and enjoy.

[1]   This is inaccurate, since animals do not rape. The implication in this answer is that rape is a 'natural instinct,' which only 'civilization' can overcome. In fact, it is our 'civilization' that has created the concept and encouraged it.

[2]   Darwin's theory concerned selection between different species, not within species. This is a misunderstanding and misuse of the concept of 'survival of the fittest'.

[3]   Pornography much more frequently shows women rather than men being dominated, tortured and humiliated. Sadism against women is a cultural theme for the West that goes back to the 'witch' burnings of the Middle Ages during which several million women were killed.

[4]   Most men do not look at pornography with a woman, as most women do not like the way women are portrayed in pornography. Also, men looking at pornography together also find that it is another way of proclaiming one's masculinity for other men to see and a way for men to have sexual feelings together while still focused on a 'heterosexual' object.

Chapter Six

Who Are Men Today?

The last twenty-five years are thought of as an era of change for women, but men have been changing too. How much have men 'undefined' their ideas of masculinity, who a real man is – and how much are men carrying on with an old point of view dressed up in a new style? Many men have a perpetual sense that 'the party is going on somewhere else', that they are missing out, that they might die without ever having really lived. (Clearly, being 'masculine' is not the most satisfying way of life.) Although most believe in equality for women, they simultaneously worry that the Brave New World 'run by women' won't have a place for them. They feel subliminally anxious and guilty because perhaps they benefit from a system of male privilege – although this guilt may be hidden or unacknowledged. Amidst such pressures, many are inclined to revolt and cry out, 'Hell with it, I can't do anything right, I'm going to act like the mean macho maverick I really am deep down!'

But most men don't really identify with such warrior images and worry that they won't live up to them. Questions men ask themselves: is a 'real man' monogamous or not? A 'good husband and father' or not? Married or single, lover or husband? While most men somehow believe in marriage, ironically most also believe they should be free, less 'tied down' and many fault themselves for not being sure what they really want. Images of mythic masculinity are not the great gift to men they may at first appear to be.

This inner turmoil means that many men today are quietly staging a revolution inside themselves, questioning the beliefs they were brought up with, redesigning their inner value system – for example, men in the business world are now rethinking the importance of work versus private life, asking how much time should be spent at work and at home, asking themselves: 'what is the meaning of life?'

Men should not blame themselves for feeling confused! After all, most boys are subjected to taunts or bullying (even being beaten up) by bigger boys or older male members of the family – 'Don't be a sissy, grow up and be a man!' – this causes boys to undergo a powerful process of attempting to conform to 'male norms' or at least outwardly seem to conform. I propose that what we call 'male nature' is in fact thus carefully constructed and manicured by our social mores, more than by biology or 'hormones', as is often claimed. Current popular clichés with a 'biological determinist' slant imply that a man's nature can't change: that men are destined biologically – via testosterone? – to be competitive and aggressive, to bond together with other men in groups excluding women, who are 'destined by biology' to be 'different', i.e., less adventurous, preferring home, and that this 'unchangeable human nature in their genes' makes them lust to be warriors and hunters, fight battles, 'fuck women'. Yet is this true? Or is this the culture trying to program men?

During the last two decades, books on 'personal growth' ('self-help' for women and 'business secrets' for men) helped individuals think through issues of identity-change. Most men no longer want the 'traditional manhood' of the past but a new way of life that they are inventing now, engaged in a momentous interior transformation that has as yet to go public.

Men and Love

Many men wrote lengthy answers to Hite's research questions; thirty of these replies were reproduced in *The Hite Report on Male Sexuality*, two are reproduced here.

Man #1:

I am a twenty-nine-year-old white male, living off and on with my lover. I work as an electrician. Every day is a real struggle, both with work and with our relationship together, but I love her and we have the best sex life I've ever had – the greatest. I've been thinking a lot about my life lately, being together so intensely with my lover has made me have a lot of thoughts, but none of the men I know ever talk about these things. That's why I'm answering this questionnaire. I would really like to know how other men feel, and I want to tell about myself

For me, being in love is not exactly the fairy-tale, sugar coated, happily-ever-after story of the movies, novels and 'great' moments in history. At times it has been painful, and a lot of times I have felt unsure of what was going on and my role in it.

When I was in my teens I thought love always implied settling down, getting married, having children, and me getting a job and supporting the lot of them, like my father and grandfather before me. It meant sacrificing one's true feelings to put on the appearance of being happy all the time. I also believed that marriage was inevitable, as everyone just gets married finally and forgets about what they really want to do. This idea of marriage is security-oriented rather than passion-oriented. I guess I really disliked the idea of traditional marriage on many levels, but felt like a weirdo for not liking it. I thought there was something wrong with me for not liking the 'normal' way of life for couples.

However... I found myself feeling lots of new feelings when I got my lover.

When we first met I had decided never to go out with, or get involved with anybody again, as it was always such a nightmare in the past, including one very difficult relationship which ended in disaster. But I felt this unbelievable sexual, physical and personality attraction to this woman as soon as I met her. We did not get involved physically for a couple of months, although I fantasized about her since the day we met. I was extremely afraid of getting involved, because I thought it would be painful, complicated and wouldn't last. However, she was so irresistible and sexy I couldn't control myself. I have never desired someone's body as much as I desire hers. I can never believe how exciting it is when we make love. I've never felt so many emotions before.

When I fell in love with her I felt as if I had discovered my emotions – but immediately I was also in turmoil. Although she made me feel alive and exhilarated and more sexually excited than I ever thought I could get and made me experience all kinds of feelings that I didn't know I had, this 'great love' also made me fear obligations. I was afraid. When my lover told me she needed me, I got scared, because I thought a lot was expected of me. (Now I understand that 'I need you' just means 'I love you' to my lover. She means 'I need to love you.' It doesn't mean she expects anything from me at all – it means 'Let me love you, loving you makes me feel good.') I thought that now I would have to be a 'husband' like my father and tied to her. The result was

115

the relationship was very rocky because I felt so torn between my lover and my ideas of obligation, duty, etc. I felt that I was getting into something really serious, something that demanded a great deal of sacrifice from me. At times it seemed burdensome, so I would rebel against this feeling of restriction by saying or doing something to hurt her, since I thought she was the cause of my tension. Really it was not her expectations of me but my idea of her expectations of me that was burdensome. I assumed she needed me and me only – that only I could fulfil her needs, and that I was trapped, because she said she loved me.

I also assumed she couldn't hurt me, or wouldn't hurt me, even if I hurt her. I refused to believe she was in control of her life and could solve her problems without me or that she could leave me if I made her unhappy. It's funny I thought this way because she is independent and successful, more than I am. I didn't want to believe that she could hurt me if she wanted to, or could break up with me, or could reject me. I didn't want to accept that she could do this – I didn't want to accept her as an equal (emotionally), and I didn't want to be vulnerable. (But I wanted her to be vulnerable.) But if you want to really feel close to somebody you must become vulnerable. It's the chance you have to take.

It's funny how men have these stereotypes of what women need. The men who have the most rigid stereotypes are the ones who have never really been close to a woman. Some of them are married to women they don't even know – they only know who they want to believe she is – they know their image of her, not her – they never ask her who she is.

Men think they please women by just being around and letting the woman please them. They can't really love a woman because they either put her on a pedestal or treat her like a mommy or a child. Very condescending no matter how you look at it. The way I was raised and brought up to be really arrogant, I thought I was God's gift to women. Men think of themselves as being really interesting – everyone is interested in what they have to say – people want to listen to them. But who wants to listen to a woman?

Most men's mothers treated them like kings, and so men feel like any other woman should too. Certainly it's not worth fighting very much with a woman to make the relationship better, since another woman will be glad to please me – at least that's the way I used to think. But fighting with my lover helped me develop as a person. Even though the fights were terrible, really, I felt I was growing in an important way. It's really precious to know someone so closely.

Every time I decided to give up my lover, I became physically ill and couldn't eat, my stomach felt like it had been stomped on, and I had tension headaches. Finally I realized that I need her love – she makes me feel happy, warm, alive – like living and doing positive things rather than negative things. I need her, and I need her love, and I want to show her that I love her any way I can because the thought of being alone again is the worst thing I can imagine right now. It's funny, because before I met her I thought I was happy alone.

One thing I never knew about before her was clitoral stimulation. I used to think that my role was to have an orgasm. I thought I should fuck until I had an orgasm, or my performance would not be up to par – I thought she could feel my orgasm. I thought it would disappoint her if I didn't have an orgasm. I thought I wasn't a man if I didn't have orgasms. Fucking would make me sweat, and make my beard grow faster! Furthermore, I thought the very best possible thing was to orgasm simultaneously – and I would time my orgasm till she had hers (during coitus) and try to come at the same time she did. I thought any vaginal spasms were the contractions of female orgasms – they felt great to me. I was sure (at the time – this is with an ex-lover) that I knew when she was orgasming, and thought she knew when I was (she could feel the hot sperm, I thought), even though we didn't ask each other very often. I never masturbated her to orgasm – I didn't know how to, didn't ask, I thought sticking a finger in her vagina was masturbating her. Sometimes during intercourse I realized she didn't orgasm. I would feel that I didn't fuck as good that day (or long enough), but I believed that intercourse was the only way to achieve female orgasm – the only right way! So I felt I had let her down, but we never discussed it, we just went to sleep. The thing I have worried about since we broke up is whether or not she had orgasms as often as I assumed she did, and also whether she liked them regularly, as some of the women in *The Hite Report* said they did. At the time my masculinity and ego would have been miniaturized beyond comprehension and I'm sure I would have developed a huge complex if I thought I wasn't giving her orgasms.

When I read that women usually didn't orgasm from intercourse, my face fell – imagine that – I believed all this time that I could given women an orgasm by fucking them – suddenly this fundamental belief of mine was shattered, and I wondered if women had been faking it all along or what. I felt helpless and really embarrassed upon learning this. I had been taking this huge credit for giving women orgasms when I didn't even know how to! It seems so funny now, but it was really a crisis when I found this out. A complete ego crisis. Not only was my ego shot, but now I had to face the problem of how to give my lover an orgasm.

The first time my lover asked me to give her an orgasm, she told me to hold my hand in a fist and put it on her pubic mound and to move it. I wasn't in a real comfortable position. But I had read *The Hite Report* at that point, so I wanted to try. Even though if you read the book you think you know a lot, but, still, to actually do it is really interesting because I'd never felt anyone's body that way before. She had shown me exactly what to do, which was so straightforward, all of a sudden I felt really enlightened.

But I also felt nervous because I kept changing the rhythm and wasn't doing it the same way all the time. I'd speed it up and slow it down and move in different directions. Then she told me not to do it like that. I started feeling kind of insecure, because I thought, well, I don't know if I'm really doing this right, plus I couldn't anticipate when she was going to have an orgasm – I didn't know how long I was going to have to keep doing this. I didn't know if I was doing it right, I didn't know if someone else could do it better than me, or what. My confidence was on the line. I felt if I didn't do it good, if I fucked…if I couldn't do it, she could easily humiliate me for not knowing how to do it by criticizing me, like 'Hey, man, haven't you ever done this before?' or 'You're not doing it right at all!' She didn't say anything. She just moved my hand back down there and told me to just do one thing, don't move around. Even though I was getting kind of worried, don't get me wrong, I really loved it! Since it was the very first time I was doing it, I was trying to make sure I was doing it right. But the thing that was really exciting was that she showed me exactly what to do – that meant she was very excited too, excited enough to want me to do it to her. It made me feel really close to her and special since nobody ever did that before – really intimate, because I always thought of masturbation as a very private thing. If she wanted me to masturbate her, that seemed really private. I felt, how could we be any closer?

Men never talk about masturbating women, at least I've never heard them talk about it. They talk about women masturbating them a lot, but they never talk about themselves masturbating women, or there being thirty-two different ways women masturbate! And I didn't even know one. I thought women masturbated by putting something inside. Masturbation had still for me a real pejorative context, like it's not the real thing, or that's just what women would do when they don't have a man. A frustrated woman would want to stick something in her, I thought, but it could never be as good as a cock. I guess that's why men think that a woman needs a man, that she could never masturbate herself as well as a man could – I've heard that said so many times. But really, a woman can just put a vibrator or her hand on her mons and just come and come and come.

Anyway, getting back to the first time I gave her clitoral stimulation, after a while when I kept trying, she was really excited and breathing heavy, her whole body was tensing up with her legs tight together and straight out – and then she got really tense and tight and moaned and held herself like that for a few minutes. Then she told me she came. It was a revelation for me.

Of all the things we had done before that – like when we were kissing and I could hear her moaning, her head is right by my ear sometimes, and I'm listening and I can feel her breathing – never was it that exciting, it was so thrilling during her orgasm. I felt like she was really strong! That was my first reaction to the whole thing – that she had a tremendous strength – a really powerful energy that was inside her. Also I felt really small next to her when she had an orgasm and I didn't!

I also felt like – well, I used to believe that the idea was to flack until you both had orgasms together, but all of a sudden I realized it was a really good feeling to enjoy someone else's orgasm, even if I didn't have one. Plus, to discover that she could have one that made me envious – plus I think she had another one about a minute later – well, I was really amazed! Later, after we did it a lot, I really got to enjoy it. She feels energetic and powerful and independent when she orgasms, and it makes me feel good to be next to someone so strong and active and alive.

Do you know the difference between being next to a really passive person and someone that's really excited? It makes me feel great, it makes me fees really excited, aroused, like having orgasms, really strong, it makes me feel like an animal. I just want to hop on and screw her at that point, and I often do.

But I consider my masturbating her one of the major things that we do. I don't consider it as a warm-up thing. Sometimes when we don't do it I miss doing it. Sometimes she's said things to me while I'm doing it that make me feel really good, or really hot. I get sweaty when I'm doing it, and I like that feeling a lot. I'll usually be really close against her body while I'm doing it, so I'll rub myself on her or I'll rub myself on the bed, or if my arm is in the right position I can rub it on my arm. I feel really wild when she's having the orgasm – she feels really wild to me, like she's breaking away from all physical restraints of any kind.

119

I've never told my friends or anybody else any of this. I never tell the guys much of anything I do. I don't know what their reactions would be. But, since most of the guys I know are always boasting about their exploits and I never do, then they boast all the more because they think I'm a prude, because I don't talk about my sex life.

But if I told them about this whole clitoral stimulation thing, they'd probably just say it's 'kinky'. Or couldn't she make it any other way? They'd probably be really freaked out because I've never heard anybody tell a story like that. I don't think most men know how to do it, and then the ones who do would be afraid to be ridiculed for talking about it. It seems like all men ever talk about is how they fuck. It would make me very nervous to talk about clitoral stimulation to the guys. When you're working with other men, for example, the first topic that comes up during the lunch break is 'Wow, I really fucked a lot last night!' Somebody will start boasting about what he's done, and then they expect you to come up with an equally macho story – the more graphic, the better, of course. And I never do come up with any stories. Then they think you can't get laid, or you're too sensitive or whatever. They don't like to talk about it in emotional terms. Of course, mostly they're not talking about their wives – sometimes they are, but usually they're trying to say they are having affairs with somebody. Most of the time they are bragging, they are also bragging that they are seeing more than one person. But sometimes people will say, 'I'm going home to fuck my wife!' I've heard that. I thought it was really nice when I heard it. It was somebody that I didn't know very well, and he said, 'I'm going home and fuck my wife!' (He was really drunk.) It sounded like a great thing to do. I should have wished him a happy time. But most men seem to think that anything outside of intercourse is a deviation from the norm, or it's not the 'real thing'. All I know is, that seems to me now like a really limited way of seeing things.

Another thing I've always heard was that you weren't supposed to have sex when the woman was having her period. Women are always supposed to hide it and not let anyone know they're having it, and men aren't supposed to know about it, and everyone is supposed to pretend like it doesn't happen.

One time we were making out, lying in bed, she didn't have any clothes on, and we were thinking about intercourse, but she still had the Tampax in. I said I wanted to take it out for her. She was going to take it out herself in the bathroom, and then wash herself, but I wanted to take it out. And it was really sexy to take it out. I wanted to look at it while it was coming out – not just reach around and pull it out – I wanted to watch it, I wanted to see the colours on it. I thought it would be really great to look at it and watch the thing come out. It seemed really beautiful to watch it come out. It was part of her on the Tampax – I just wanted to watch it, I don't know why. It was really sexy. When I took it out I had it and I didn't want to throw it away. I wanted to keep it. It smelled good. So I put it in my mouth. It was great to be chewing on it, tasting it.

It smelled strong but it smelled really good, it was really sexy the way it smelled, plus it was part of her. It smelled sweaty, kind of, a sharp and kind of sweaty smell, just like regular blood and mucus together, but also with some kind of a sharp, strong odour – the more, the better.

It is very exciting to just mess around sometimes. I like kissing, squeezing, my cock fondled and stroked, I like to be licked, and stroked on the neck and back and be bitten on the chest. I like to be sucked. We both make advances, because we both love to mess around. If I want to get her excited, I make an advance. When she makes an advance, it gets me very excited.

I love to masturbate my lover to orgasm and feel her tremble when she orgasms. But also just caring for her is lots of fun. I like to give massages to my lover and bathe her. I wasn't raised to do this – quite the contrary – I was raised to keep distant from others physically.

If I'm with my lover I sometimes have orgasms, sometimes not. Making love doesn't require having orgasm to be beautiful. I like to get more and more excited and to stay like that. Why end it? The building up of feelings is much more exciting than having an orgasm and going to sleep. My lover often drives me crazy, to the point that my desires get very strong and uncontrollable. I love her for making me feel that excited. I crave her, need her, and it feels great to really want someone like that – it makes me feel real, alive. I like to get my desire build up to a frenzy. It gets painful, it's such a gnawing, craving desire. As the excitement builds up, we get rougher. Orgasms that come from frenzy are the best – they are uncontrollable. This is very different from 'timing my orgasm with hers' – what a conceited practice – and boring! My lover doesn't orgasm from intercourse, but she is a great fuck, because she makes me crave her. I want to flick her in every part of her body, and cream all over her. To feel this way is the best feeling in the world.

I love intercourse. It feels great physically. Emotionally it is very satisfying and soothing. We have intercourse several times a week. Sometimes I come very soon upon entering, and it feels good when this happens involuntarily.

But I'd rather build up the excitement. Knowing that I don't have to make her orgasm from intercourse makes intercourse less traumatic, and I don't feel obligated to orgasm myself I can enjoy being inside her for various lengths of time and go back in later and do other things meanwhile.

I have only orgasmed once from fellatio. It is very pleasant but too gentle to orgasm. I need harder pressure to orgasm, or a huge amount of penis stimulation beforehand to orgasm this way. I love it when my lover masturbates me, but it takes a long time to bring me to orgasm. I like my balls rubbed, and a finger up my ass sometimes.

The first time my lover stuck a finger up my ass, it hurt and felt good simultaneously. I didn't really like it; it made me feel like a little baby being punished and brought tears to my eyes. But it also felt sort of like an orgasm – a continuous orgasm, not like a regular quick, pleasurable, painless ejaculation. Sometimes it feels like I am regressing to childhood – I feel like I am unlearning sphincter control, because sphincter discipline is the definition of being an individual, a responsible person. With a finger up my ass, I feel utterly helpless, like a child, like I can't control my shitting, like my partner has complete control over me. Ironically it is very pleasurable. I feel completely out of control, compared to intercourse, where I feel in control, powerful, like a man, an adult, in control of my body. And penetration makes me feel free and like I am being filled.

I usually have at least two orgasms a day from masturbation if I'm alone. Sometimes I masturbate one to five times a day, usually two to three. I like to do it, but I don't talk about it much. It relieves tension, but it makes me a little depressed later. I like it because it is a quick way to have an orgasm. I don't like it because it doesn't really satisfy me or make me happy, the way making love does.

To be a man means to come out on top. Or like my mother used to say: 'I don't care what you are, just be the best at whatever you do.' Competition begins at an early age – kindergarten, where kids try to outdo each other in everything they do. Of course, the boys have boy games and girls have girl games. The emphasis is on excelling: who can run fastest, play harder, play rougher. I always felt insecure about it, because I wasn't very aggressive and didn't want to be – on the physical level, that is. I was deathly afraid of getting into a fight. I was paranoid all the time that somebody would pick a fight with me. In order to survive, I had to develop and excel somehow. So in grade school I excelled in my classes. At least people respected me from being smart in class.

It seems like people love to take out their frustration and hatred for the system on an individual who doesn't succeed. Especially in high school, where individuals are outright ostracized for dressing 'funny,' being slow, being quiet, introverted, 'square', 'prudish', 'ugly', fat, you name it, the group can tease someone to death. I survived a lot of this somehow, and now I've even learned to get the group's respect – but I feel really bad that this harassment and pressure is so prevalent. I've seen guys actually drop out of school because the rest of the class teased them so much.

This cruel quality in men seems to be a big part of masculinity – to be able to inflict pain on weaker, slower individuals is the tough, macho way to show your superiority. Men justify cruelty by emphasizing that the victim is a 'weak' person, who deserves it. And this mentality also says, 'Why not? I deserve everything I got, I earned it – the slobs deserve everything they get too (punishment).' I don't understand this competition fully, except I do know it is prevalent in every aspect of my life, and I do it myself too. But I hate it – I feel 'on guard' all the time around other men.

Only men work where I work – lately we are repairing dangerous telephone wires and lines that have been cut, etc. and other electrical wiring. The most macho ones are the meanest, sweatiest, most foulmouthed, drink more beer, smoke bigger cigars and tell the 'dirtiest' jokes, very abusive towards women. When a woman passes by where we are working, every man becomes self-conscious of his macho image. They light up a cigarette, stop working and stare at her, undress her mentally, very aware that the others are doing the same thing and will nod to each other if she is sexy or make a face if they don't think she is. Men in groups are hostile, edgy and like to show that they don't have feelings – feelings of tenderness, caring, or friendship (except under the rules of bonding), or feelings of pain, be it emotional or physical. Men pride themselves among each other on their ability to not flinch while in pain. Many jobs we do involve exposure to dangerous live wires, or require us to work at dangerous heights, but most macho men won't wear safety equipment unless it is required or the situation is extremely dangerous, because macho men like to show each other that they don't feel any pain.

Macho men comment to each other about female passers-by, and if you don't have a comment to support the group's opinion you are considered (1) a fag, (2) a mama's boy, (3) a prude, (4) a real jerk, (5) a jerk-off. Then you draw the next round of insults from the group and become the victim of their further abuses and hostile comments. It's very childlike, the way children ostracize and tease the kid with glasses or a stutter or any physical weakness. The thing is, this whole macho group-bonding thing is actually taught in the high schools and trade schools, as the students who are studying skilled trades like plumbing and electricity and carpentry must also withstand the non-stop group harassment and teasing that goes on in the classroom. Even the instructors do it, and humiliate or abuse slow or weak students. 'You gotta be a real man to get into the Brotherhood of the Plumbers Union!' To keep a job one must deal with this horrible social system. The foreman is typically the very most macho, grouchy, cursing, angry-looking person on the site. There is never any positive reinforcement for good work, only criticism for bad or slow work. One never admits ignorance in one's job just as one never does about women, because that would bring the roof down on your own head and all the humiliation that goes with it.

Most of the men I work with get paid very well for their work and resent women who try to break in as equals. They really don't want women as equals, only as a fuck or a 'mommy' or a cute daughter. They want to protect the 'poor things', be a big hero all the time and bring home more money than the women. Men act very different among themselves than they do in groups with women. They don't talk about women among themselves as equals or humans – they say stuff like 'She likes cock', 'She's frigid' and especially 'She loves my ass'. They don't say, 'I love her', 'I respect her', 'I need her' or 'I hope she is feeling good'. The worst part of it is that I don't do anything to change this really. I just put up with their attitudes because I want the money. And to be perfectly honest, I also want to be accepted.

My father always expected the women of the family to do certain daily things, like clean the house, cook, take care of the children, and the boys and men to do other, more special things, like shovel snow, fix cars, clean the garage and basement. I'm sure he expects me to know more about the world than my wife and to make more money than her. He believes his role is to support the family and wife. He's worked seven days a week, fourteen hours a day (as a plant maintenance supervisor) to do this since I can remember. He doesn't spend time with his family. I never got to know my father till I began working with him. He is a workaholic and doesn't understand how anyone feels about anything. I hate him but I also love him very much. My mother always listened to me, and trusted me to make my own decisions, even though we never talked heart to heart or were never really physically close.

It was my sister I was really close to (one year older). She was my 'best friend' in second, third and fourth grades. We did things together as equals with no sexual (role) barriers. We were friends. As a child I remember that boys were supposed to play with boys' toys and girls with girls' toys. Girls played 'house', 'dolls', and 'shopping', and boys played army men, fort games, snowball fights and more strenuous games. But there were some games that boys and girls could play together, like cards and table games, ride bikes. There were times when I felt torn between playing with my sister, who was my best friend, and playing with the boys. Especially skating – the girls did figure skating, and the boys played hockey. Of course, it was an honour to be accepted into the group of boys as a hockey player; I remember feeling like I had betrayed my sister when I went to the rink with her but didn't play with her once we got there. I didn't want to be a sissy, so I let her play with her girlfriends and I played with the boys.

It was never the same after that. We took off on our respective masculine and feminine roles. As an adult, it is almost impossible for a man to be 'friends' with a woman or 'best friends'. The roles we are assigned don't allow it. Men have their wives, and their friends (other men). Men don't see women as equals; perhaps they did as children, but when they follow their roles, they begin to feel guilt for leaving women behind and later feel contempt for women who are not their equals, since they didn't let them be. Men show contempt for women because they are not able to treat them with respect and honesty, because they consider themselves superior.

My lover is a feminist – and I respect her for it. She is honest and courageous. She won't stand to be treated like a second-class person. She is very strong. But I used to think that the Women's Movement was a minority of women radicals who were very bitter people, who were overly critical of society, and generally too extreme to be taken seriously. I never thought of it as if I were a woman, nor did I ever experience what it's like to be a woman, to be stared at by men, discriminated against on the job level, the educational level and even in conversation. Feminists made me nervous: I felt I was innocent – I never intentionally was unfair to women – I was nice to them – why should they be mad at me?

Of course, I didn't understand. The weird thing is that even though I wasn't satisfied with society's definition of me as a 'man', I was not inspired by the group of women who were rebelling against the society's definition of them as women.

I have discovered that the most important thing for keeping our relationship on an even keel is a daily sharing of feelings, how we feel. I never grew up thinking this was important. I thought I was always supposed to be objective, and that I should suppress any other feelings, to express them would be weak. One result of this was that, sometimes she would get very angry and upset because I didn't express my feelings to her. Other times, too, she would tell me her feelings about something that had happened, but I just sat silently and she would get mad. When she got upset at me I felt very nervous, upset, afraid, angry, mean, and confused. But I never expressed this either, nor did I ask her why she felt so angry. My basic impulse was just to get out of that situation; I wanted to avoid situations in which I felt anything other than loved, confident, wanted, happy, and stable. I thought her anger was just a waste of time. I thought to myself, 'I love her – doesn't she understand that? Why doesn't she let me love her?'

It really helped when I finally realized that communication about feelings and moods is something that has to be kept up every day. Even now, if we are not really communicating and keeping in touch and sharing with each other how we feel, I get confused, estranged and insecure about where I stand. Then I get paranoid and pretend that everything is OK, instead of saying the truth, like 'I feel weird, we're drifting apart. Why? Aren't I communicating, or aren't you?'

I answered this because I want to know how other men feel about these things. I haven't been able to talk these things over with anybody, and they are very important to me. And at the same time, I also found it a relief to say I find some of my friends' behaviour really revolting sometimes. But I could never say this to their faces. It's really crazy, but at the same time I like them.

Man #2:

At age seventy, with the awareness that death and oblivion are much closer now than ever before, I have become much more conscious of the essential loneliness of the human condition and of an increasing desire for a warm, close and loving relationship with another person, and, for me as of now, sex is an essential component of such a relationship. The physiological aspects of sex and achievement of orgasm, while still very enjoyable, are not as strong or compelling a part of my sex life as formerly, while the psychological components as expressed in hugging, kissing and caressing are now much more important. In retirement, with the interests and challenges of my work no longer demanding my concern, my need for this latter type of sex seems to have greatly increased.

My wife and I have been married thirty-nine years, during most of which we struggled to overcome a sexual incompatibility deriving from our mutual ignorance of female sexuality.

From adolescence on, my wife has been obsessed with the conviction, probably derived from the many romantic novels that she has read, that the highest peak of sexual ecstasy that a woman can reach is in experiencing a vaginal orgasm, and any woman who goes through life without having them has only half lived. She has also long been convinced that the main obstacle to her achievement of this blissful experience was my inability to maintain an erection and continue 'pumping' indefinitely. Having a smaller than average penis, I was preconditioned to feelings of inadequacy, and with no basis for disputing her faith in vaginal orgasms (*The Hite Report on Female Sexuality* came thirty-five years too late to salvage our sex life!), our sexual encounters became sessions of frustration, bitter recriminations, and mutual hostility so distasteful that I eventually became impotent and we stopped having sex altogether.

I am white, in good health, and the father of three grown children. My parents were of the lower middle class with only grade-school educations. They were loving and moderately religious. I have an MA in chemistry, worked thirty-six years for a major oil company doing technical work that I enjoyed, retired, taught chemistry in school for a few years and again retired. In religion I am a humanist. I had no sexual experiences until around age twenty-two, when I finally rejected the brainwashing of my parents regarding the terrible effects of 'playing with oneself' and began to masturbate regularly.

After marriage to my wife, a sexually quite inhibited woman, the sequence of operations gradually evolved to include (1) imbibing two or three cocktails to relax my wife's inhibitions, (2) insertion of a diaphragm by my wife, (3) pre-play in the form of kisses and caresses applied to various supposedly sensitive areas of my wife's head and body, (4) finger or tongue massage (usually the former with which she felt less embarrassment) of the clitoris to near or incipient orgasm, (5) hasty mounting 'missionary' style and thrusting in and out with the penis in a consistently unsuccessful effort to convert the near-orgasm to what my wife has always firmly believed must be the epitome of ecstasy for any woman, but after thirty-nine years of trying has not yet achieved: a vaginal orgasm, (6) rapid fading of my wife's sexual excitement of the near-orgasm to a feeling of bitter disappointment and frustration while I pumped away and eventually had my orgasm, the pleasure of which, however, was tempered by the knowledge that I had somehow again failed to achieve for my wife the one thing that she felt was essential for a woman's happiness, (7) finger massage of the clitoris to complete (although sometimes only simulated) orgasm, and (8) a 'post-mortem' of the operation which usually constituted the final scene of this little comedy-tragedy, with my wife, sometimes in tears, agonizing over her failure once again to attain vaginal orgasm and ascribing the failure at times to some lack within herself, at times to my inability to continue the in-and-out thrusting indefinitely on the chance that her sexual excitement might eventually again be stimulated to the desired orgasm. Gradually these always disappointing and, for me, guilt-laden sexual encounters acquired such consistently negative associations that they became distasteful to me, I had increasing difficulty obtaining erections, and eventually, after thirty-nine years of married life, became impotent.

Although my sex life with my wife has always been very unsatisfactory to both of us, in other respects we enjoy a good, even if unexciting relationship. In fact, aside from our sexual difficulties, our married life has been surprisingly harmonious, and it is especially so now that we are no longer fighting 'the battle of the sexes'. I think I can truly say that we still respect and love each other in a nonsexual way.

I am quite sure that, although I was in love several times before marriage and a few times (at a distance) since, I have never been as deeply in love as I am right now with my lover. Not too long ago, at my suggestion, we adopted open marriage and now my wife at age sixty-five has a 'young' lover in his forties with whom she can continue to pursue her will-o'-the-wisp, the vaginal orgasm, and I have found a warm, hugging, kissing, caressing, oral-sex-oriented woman who has revitalized my sex life and with whom I have fallen deeply in love. Although of very different backgrounds and with a sixteen-year difference in our ages, we seem to be made for each other in the unprecedented degree to which our tastes, interests, likes and dislikes, coincide. I'm in seventh heaven while we're together and miss her terribly when we're apart. I certainly never expected to fall so deeply in love at this age! It's a moot question whether the delights of being together outweigh the pain of separation and the near-hopelessness of our ever being able to get together permanently. However, I find our relationship very deeply satisfying emotionally, and it adds a whole new dimension to my life. Also, as she says, the delightful periods that we do spend together are like a permanent honeymoon taken on the instalment plan, with the periods of separation ensuring the permanence of our enchantment with each other. My relationship with my lover is essentially a monogamous one on my part, although not on hers, since she still has sex with her husband.

As I grow older, I find that the greatest pleasure in sex, for me, is the feeling of closeness or 'oneness' with my loved one that it gives me. I enjoy being touched and kissed because the sensual pleasure and feeling of intimacy is more prolonged. Still, although having orgasms is not as important to me now at age seventy as when I was younger, they are important. I certainly would feel deprived if my partner did not help me to an orgasm every other day or so of our lovemaking, if only as a demonstration of her concern that I should get as much pleasure as possible.

I enjoy masturbation when I am separated from my loved one and feel 'in the mood'. When we are separated, I may masturbate from one to three times per week. Masturbation with me always leads to orgasm. I usually masturbate in the shower, with a hard jet of hot water hitting against the underside of my penis. I usually fantasize variations of cunnilingus.

I enjoy cunnilingus with any woman sexually attractive enough that I could enjoy kissing her on the mouth, but even more with the woman I deeply love. The pleasure is both physical in the warmth and softness of her parts and the stimulating 'femaleness' of the taste and odour, and psychological in that cunnilingus comes closer than anything else to satisfying the strong desire I have for attaining the greatest possible intimacy with her. Another important and pleasurable aspect of cunnilingus is the intense satisfaction I feel when my partner achieves orgasm, as she normally does.

I also very much enjoy fellatio and always orgasm this way. Even at age seventy I'm sure that I could orgasm every day this way if I had the opportunity. However, since my lover and I are only able to get together for two or three days at a time and only in the daytime, these occurrences are limited to two or three times every week or so. With my lover's fellatio, I never have difficulty having an orgasm.

With a new partner whom I love, ejaculation is just one episode in an extended period of loving and caressing. In a shallow, physical sense I feel momentarily satisfied, but in a much deeper sense I have the feeling that I could never really be fully satisfied unless our bodies could somehow be melted and fused together into a single unified being. For me kissing, hugging and caressing seem to bring me closer to this ideal state than simply ejaculating. This life is a very lonely place when one has no one with whom to share human closeness and warmth and love, and for me the sense of mutual caring and concern are much more important than a mere orgasm.

So who is the modern man? Obviously there are many answers to this question. Not all modern men take drugs like Viagra or fear senility, but there are a number of observations we can make about what the modern man thinks sex is and what he thinks about women and love.

Do Men Believe in Love?

Descriptions of being in love – the following written by two young men – often imply that intense feelings of being in love with a woman are unwanted, after their early experiences with their mothers and society have taught them to avoid intense sexual emotions at all costs – and to define 'real love' as something less passionately involving, perhaps a feeling even divorced from 'sex'.

'When she finally broke it off it was as if I had died. It was the only time in my life that I ever cried myself to sleep at night, and this I did frequently. I did not actually consciously think about suicide but I considered myself already dead. A greater emptiness and sense of loss I have not known. Since that time I have not been able to love a woman with such utter abandonment. I just haven't been able to do it. This happened twelve years ago and I can still feel the pain. If I were to see her right now I know my heart would jump into my throat.'

'There is the good kind of love, but then there is the other kind, the kind that can't or won't work for whatever reasons. Nothing makes sense. It's completely unexpected, even unwanted. Who in hell would want to feel jealous? Or possessive? But that's all part of it. The feeling is like: I want this person so much it makes me feel guilty for wanting too much. But this is what keeps me going, it's what I live for and think about every day. I think that maybe today it will all work, even though I know this is foolishness. And that makes me feel bad too, like I'm feeling something I'm not supposed to because it isn't shared, but I feel it anyway.'

Most Men Don't Marry the Women They Most Passionately Love

This is perhaps the most important finding of my research into men's psychosexuality, published partly in *The Hite Report on Male Sexuality*. Not only do most men not marry the women they most passionately love or desire they also feel proud of having controlled themselves and 'chosen rationally'. The real surprise is that most men not only do not marry the women they most passionately love but they also remain proud of this, proud that they 'keep control' – even though they regret their 'lost love'. Why?

Traditionally, men have been taught not to take love that seriously – not to let a woman 'run' their life. But clearly men do fall passionately in love, experience all the feelings of ecstasy and abandon, all the happiness that goes with it – for at least two weeks. At an early point, many men become very confused and apprehensive. Being brought up not to let themselves be 'out of control', or 'overly-emotional', men mistrust the excitement, the rush, and want to rid themselves of the feelings that are sweeping over them, feelings they are not proud of.

Men's comments about these feelings are quite illuminating. 'To be in love,' as one man in his early twenties writes, 'is to be uncomfortable because you are out of control, you do things you wouldn't normally do. Women are more willing to be dependent, or part of another person, than a man who wants to keep a separation, keep himself for himself, who fears losing his independence. Of course, one does sometimes start to fall in love, but you can always stop it before it's too late. It will be nice in the future if they invent a pill to neutralize you if you fall in love – to alleviate your dis-ease!'

Most men are so uncomfortable with feelings of love, desire, need and vulnerability that they do not marry the woman they are most 'in love' with. Distrusting the feelings, they run from their own emotional openness, and furthermore, are proud that they 'made the right decision', 'didn't let their feelings carry them away' and 'stayed in control' – made a 'rational decision'. They are proud and feel they did the right thing, marrying 'more sensibly'.

And yet this, added to the fact that most men are brought up not to respect women – other than as mothers or mothering-type, helping figures – puts most marriages in a very vulnerable, problematic position. An additional problem is most men's training not to talk about feelings or to solve emotional problems by discussing them, talking them out: most men's reaction to a dispute would be to retain 'manly' objectivity by going for a walk, etc., expecting the air to have cleared on their return, and to feel proud of this solution, since they had not 'lost control'.

Many men in this study said that they were deeply frustrated, angry or disappointed with their emotional relationships with women, at the same time that they treasured these relationships as providing the happiest and most intimate moments of their lives.

Most men had not married the women they most passionately loved. Most men did not feel comfortable being deeply in love. Although they sounded very similar to women when they spoke of the first wonderful feelings of falling in love, very soon thereafter many began to feel uncomfortable, anxious, even trapped – and wanted to withdraw. Most men felt very out of control of their emotions when they were in love, not reasonable and 'rational', and most men did not like this feeling: men have been taught that the worst thing possible is to be out of control, to be 'overly emotional,' as this behaviour is 'womanly'.

Thus, being in love, a man begins to feel out of control, 'unmanly' and, even worse, he begins to feel that he is controlled by the woman – that is, he would do anything to please her, he is afraid of her displeasure, and so he is 'dominated' by her. This is an intolerable situation. Add to this the idea that most men still believe on some level that there are two kinds of women: 'good', motherly women, and 'bad', sexy women. The man, feeling very attracted when falling in love, is sure that he should not let himself go into his love, trust in it and count on her. At this point, he tends to pull back, to try to provoke a fight or find a problem in the relationship, in order to regain his former stance in life, his 'control'. He looks for, or believes he should look for, someone more 'stable', someone who doesn't put him in a constant position of rethinking his life. Most men described this as a 'rational' decision and took pride in having acted wisely, remaining cool and collected, and 'using their heads' – even though they missed their lost love.

Most of the men in these marriages were not monogamous. Most marriages based on this 'rational' idea tended to develop a pattern (at least in the man) of extramarital sex unknown to the woman – or, since there was such emotional distance in the marriage anyway, sometimes the wife did know but just did not care, since she herself had little interest in sex with her husband. These 'traditional' marriages, while not close in the romantic sense, could often be long-term: if reasons other than love were the basis of the marriage in the first place, it was not necessary to maintain a high level of communication, intimacy or understanding to ensure continuation of the marriage. 'Newer', more equal, marriages in which emotional closeness and equality between the man and woman were goals, tended to be more monogamous and also to have quite different sexual patterns.

Are men getting the most they can out of life, learning such definitions of 'being a man on top', or are they being short-changed?

Do Men Today Like Marriage?

Joke after joke tells us that men try to 'escape the trap of matrimony', remain 'free', that it is women who are 'desperate to get married'.

Yet statistics tells us that the majority of divorces all over the world (even those in previous centuries) are usually brought by women, not men. We have no statistics on who asks whom to get married: could it be that it is also women who are 'popping the question'? Tradition has it that this is a man's privilege and honour, to 'choose' the woman and 'ask for her hand'.

However, most married men like marriage – although they often hide this fact. For example, most men in my research say that their wife is their best friend as well as lover and that they like this close companionship. Men like long-term, stable relationships with women (why shouldn't they?), although men are normally portrayed as liking to be together with other men, as the 'norm'.

When I asked men why they like marriage, they usually mention such things as love for their wife, sleeping together in the same bed, sharing a family and a history together and making future plans. If men have complaints about marriage, they generally voice them only as complaints about a particular behaviour of their wife's, not the whole idea. Significantly, very few men indeed say that their marriage makes them feel 'tied down'; contrary to stereotype, this does not seem to be an issue. They often find that they have plenty of time and freedom to 'have sex elsewhere' if desired, or go out on their own, or go to work, etc.

Why do men hide the fact that they like marriage? Most male movie heroes and rock stars are portrayed as being single; in fact, it is hard to think of any male film heroes who portray married heroes (they may be married in real life, but not in films). Although it is simplistically said that this is because 'female fans like men single', in fact, it is mostly a male audience that dictates choices of films attended. Men especially like single male heroes who are 'free' and have adventures, admired for their gutsiness. Rock stars guard their image as non-married, 'free' and single, adventurous males. You have to be single and 'wild' to be a rock star. Male trend-phrases refer to the terror of being 'tied down to a woman', wanting to 'avoid marriage like the plague' and 'needing my freedom, my space' and so on.

Does this imply men are married against their will? That men are basically against the idea of 'family'? How do men grow to connect the idea that being 'free', being a 'real male', means not being married – or even 'too much in love'?

Usually women are blamed for the changes going on in the family, for attacking the family and demanding that it change. In fact, the rebellion against marriage and family was largely begun by men in the 1960s. Even in the 'golden age' of the family during the 1950s, jokes were commonly made by men (echoed by male comedians on television) about 'the old lady', 'my nagging wife' or 'that gold-digger, my wife.'

Men's revolt against marriage grew during and after World War II. Was this because of the 'sexual revolution' and the fact that men had more access to sex outside marriage after the advent of the birth control pill? Or were the pill and change in attitudes ('sexual revolution') more the result of men's new drive to be 'free' than its cause? During World War II, foreign travel and 'men together' may have seemed more satisfying than 'the woman waiting at home' – although men's rush home in the 1950s do not seem to show anything like this, rather the reverse.

In fact, men's drive to 'shake off the shackles of marriage' came before the 'sexual revolution': contributing to men's revolt against marriage were wartime propaganda images of men created by governments to get more men to enlist in the army for fighting. The myths governments needed to create during World War II to convince men that they wanted to enlist in the army and go to war (not stay home with their wives and loved ones) – that 'real men love combat' – changed ideas of male psychology. During the war years, the US government alone poured enormous sums of money into the Hollywood film industry. No longer were men portrayed as being happy 'getting their girl' at home; now 'real men' were those who sought adventure far from home, relishing the thrill of battle with other men at their side – or sometimes, heroically on their own.

These images of masculinity – 'man as fighting animal' (with basic instincts) – left the impression that a 'real man' is a killer, not a family man. This cliché continues in films today. Is this image wrong? No one yet has figured out completely 'the meaning of life'. Is it for a man to wander until he finds 'himself'? Or find 'enlightenment'? Or is the meaning of life for a man to join with someone else and create a family (whether the family is biological or simply an affectionate unit)? Why, even now, more than sixty years after the war, does the stereotype of 'real man as single loner' seem almost to intensify, rather than fade? Although research shows that men like marriage – the vast majority of men do marry, most do not want to divorce, and men even live longer when they sleep (sleep, whether or not they have sex) together regularly with a woman – although all the indications are that men like and need marriage or long-term positive relationships with women, still the idea of the need for 'freedom' and space' has the most cachet. Why? It is the tightness of the 'traditional family' institution that men don't like, the way marriage has been defined – not long-term relationships with women.

Are Men Monogamous?

How often have you heard jokes that make the statement: 'What can you expect from a man? Men can't help having a roving eye – it's their nature!'

Women's eyes are not expected to 'rove'; women are (or have been, at least) expected to love one man only, no matter what. People remind women today that 'not long ago' it was the custom for men to have more than one wife, and that therefore, women should realize their good fortune and not push their luck, not ask for too much!

Fortunately women today are beginning to have enough economic autonomy to declare to a man that either they will both be monogamous, or neither will be – depending on how a woman feels about her relationship. In some countries with extremist Islamic governments, a woman can be 'legitimately' killed for being 'unfaithful' – not a man, however.

Although sometimes men celebrate a monogamous love for 'one woman only', often they hide such feelings in shame. Some men are embarrassed and think they will look 'wimpy', not like a 'super-stud', if they proclaim how happy they are being monogamous. In some cultures, men are more encouraged to 'display ' their masculinity by showing how many women they can have; in others, fidelity to marriage and family are considered virtuous for a man.

One young man in my research describes how he doubted that he should 'be focused on one woman': 'I feel this unbelievable sexual, physical and personal attraction to her, and have ever since the minute I met her. She is irresistibly sexy, I can't control myself when I'm around her or I just think of her. When I see other women at work, even if they are attractive, neat bodies, etc., it's like they're not even there for me. I only want her. I never tell this to the other guys at work.'

But what if the other guys are largely putting on an act too? What if most really like being married but are afraid to say so? One older man, married thirty years, puts it this way: 'I never wanted to leave my wife, even at times when we were not so happy. Yes, there were other women along the way who attracted me, but before everything else comes my relationship with her. We are in the business of life together, I mean we have raised three children, we have seen each other at our best and worst, she is still beautiful to me and interesting. But no one believes it when I say this; they think it can't be true. So I don't talk about it much.'

So much fun has been made of men who are married ('he's henpecked', 'his wife is nagging him all the time'), rather than giving men respect and admiration for forming a good relationship with a woman that many men feel embarrassed at a tendency in themselves to be monogamous. They fight it like crazy. Even if they fall truly in love, sometimes they try – no matter how happy they are – to extricate themselves from being 'in too deeply' or 'totally committed' since they don't want to be called a 'sissy' by other men! (Or by their own inner policeman.)

This is tragic, since if a man is lucky enough to feel so much passion for someone that he doesn't want to look elsewhere for sex, he is fortunate. The old idea that decrees that 'being a man' means making lots of sexual conquests with many women, penetrating them once or twice but not thereafter being 'tied down' or 'committed' in any way, comes from a preoccupation with increasing reproduction that dates back thousands of years: some early societies trained men to feel they should 'spread as much seed as possible to prove they are men' in order to increase the population. If a man does feel deeply involved with, and attracted to, one woman, but tries not to feel it, this is unfortunate.

Many men try, when they first fall in love, according to my research, to 'lower the temperature', cool down the relationship, 'get it under control' – although they usually only succeed in confusing the other person and causing rifts. A chance for extraordinary happiness is lost. Men kill part of themselves in killing these 'wilder' feelings.

In a culture in which men are trained to graft their emotions primarily onto the system ('a man's duty', 'work comes first', 'I must go into the army', etc.), a culture in which passion for a woman is labelled one of the 'baser' parts of life, men often try to reject the passionate love they feel, going through three stages: first, feeling 'swept away'; secondly, struggling against the passion inside them to 'regain control'; third, fighting with the loved one, seeing her as the 'enemy' or 'guilty' for 'provoking too many feelings'; and (most ironic of all) 'creating a lack of stability'! This stage often leads to a break-up.

A man not allowing himself to love fully – or forcing himself to cut off his passionate feelings – can cause him to feel empty, leading to a quest for multiple partners in an attempt to satisfy an appetite that can never be satisfied without truly loving. Monogamous men are generally much happier than other men, by the way – not because they are monogamous, but because they feel like being monogamous. Because they live with someone they love and with whom they have a real relationship.

Of course, not every life – male or female – contains a 'happy ending', not everyone winds up living with the person of their dreams so that being monogamous comes naturally.

Monogamy is not always right for every part of everyone's life, but monogamy for men is at least as rewarding and satisfying as it is (or not) for women. And it allows love to grow, based on stability and time together for real closeness.

Men's Perception of Women as 'Weak'

But why does seeing women basically as 'sex partners' or mothers, or looking down on them as generally weak and inferior make men angry with women? The first reason is that this makes men feel guilty and conflicted in their loyalties and angry with women for making them feel guilty:

'Since she loves me so much, I feel guilty that maybe I don't love her as much. She really looks up to me. Sometimes I feel like she worships me. This makes me feel funny. I know that as a man it is my duty to help her, but sometimes I feel annoyed with her. Why can't she stand on her own two feet?'

'I can't help looking down on women. You can get anything you want from them by telling them they are "special". They love to be told they are "special".'

'I guess what makes me maddest about women is when they lack pride, underestimate themselves and are over-careful. When I see a woman with intelligence and abilities take a passive role in life because she lacks self-confidence, it upsets me and I tend to become critical.'

A great deal of the alienation between men and women is caused by men's knowledge, on some level, of their superior, privileged class status over women – or at least the difference in status. This is an unspoken issue, too emotionally charged to discuss in most cases, whose existence is taken for granted between most men and women, but which has a diffused effect over the entire relationship. Although men felt somewhat free to voice these feelings about their mothers, and to recognize their mothers' subordinate position *vis-à-vis* their fathers – often calling them 'weak' – many men did not feel free to express, or perhaps even recognize, some of these same feelings about their own wives and lovers.

A further problem is economics. Since the society has kept women economically, socially and even emotionally dependent on men, it is no wonder that men sometimes feel 'trapped' in marriage. And yet, most men do not explicitly connect problems with the social and legal role assigned women (or their own role as 'caretaker') and their own feeling of lack of satisfaction in marriage, or suffocation. Most seem to feel that their problems in their own marriage related to their wife as an individual, i.e., she was being unreasonable and making too many demands – or that she was not responding with a sufficient amount of affection (gratitude?) by participating in more frequent sex, etc. Or she was not being 'giving' enough. Thus, men felt perfectly justified in going outside the marriage for sex and pleasure, since they felt they were being cheated inside the marriage.

However, even though most men did not connect society's assigning women a second-class or dependent role with their own feelings of dissatisfaction, accompanied by their endless search for a gratifying 'sexual' relationship with a woman, a majority did recognize the bad effect that being supported or dependent could have on one's spirit. When asked, 'Do you envy women the choice of having someone support them, the seeming lack of pressure on them to make money?' almost no men said they envied women, and most stated strongly that they would not like to be supported by someone else.

The traditional marriage, in which the man controlled the money, while the woman's domain was the house, was the type of marriage most likely to include a pattern of extramarital sex for the man.

The happiest men in this study were those with the closest, most functioning relationships with women: that is, a minority of (in most cases, married) men. Trying to live by the male code, being totally self-sufficient, emotionally and economically, always providing shelter and food (or sex and orgasms), never receiving or needing anything, never needing a woman's love more than she needs the man's: all this hurts and stunts men.

Some men were beginning to see how their own welfare is tied up with women's fight to restructure their lives and relationships for the better – to redefine themselves above and beyond the traditional confines of 'femininity'. 'Masculinity' can be just as much of a pressure on men as an enforced 'femininity' can be on women.

But one of the deepest problems still prevalent in many men's minds is the connection they made between money and sex with women. Most men believed that women were somehow for sale. When asked, 'How do you feel about paying a woman for sex?' meaning in prostitution, many answered, 'You always pay anyway': explaining that – whether it is in marriage where the man provides support in return for (what he considers should be) domestic and sexual services, childrearing or on a date, in which the man pays for dinner, expecting sex in return – he is always paying. Many said that it was more honest, and more of a bargain, to actually pay a woman outright. In fact, the number one reason given by most men for being angry with women was financial support, mentioning frequently that you can't trust women, that women often 'use' men to get financial support. Many men feel they can never be sure that a woman loves them just for themselves – as many men said: 'Maybe she is just staying with me as a meal ticket.'

Are things changing? Do men want to redefine their relationships with women?

The inequalities between men's and women's traditional roles have placed a tremendous burden on relationships between men and women, often creating an adversary, distrusting situation. If individuals were free to choose their role in a relationship, to create new types of relationships with each other, and especially more equal relationships, there would be less need for distrust and more mutual respect and communication possible.

Since our society has kept women in a secondary position, economically and socially, most women remain somehow dependent on men. Traditionally, a woman with children had to depend on the good will of her husband for her and her children's support. This may have created a subtle pressure on her to fear her husband and to cater to his wishes, no matter what her own feelings – thus inhibiting a free and spontaneous relationship between equals.

Clearly, men have cause to be insecure about women's motives in loving them in a society in which women are dependent on men's good will and financial support for survival. Thus, keeping women economically dependent places men in a position in which they may sometimes wonder if they are loved for themselves or because they are, as one man put it, 'a meal ticket'. This is a tragic consequence of the system as we have known it – both women and men have had, in many ways, to distrust each other, and this distrust can permeate even deep and committed relationships.

And yet, many men in this study did not see the relevance to them of the Women's Movement; they did not see the connection between their own feelings of being trapped and alienated – in their role in marriage, in their jobs, in their lifestyle, their lack of closeness – and the critique of society and relationships which the women's movement poses, the suggestions the Women's Movement has made for improving things. Many men tended to see the Women's Movement more as 'women complaining, raising a ruckus' than understanding how both men and women, working to change and restructure their relationships (and the family), could make increased happiness for both. In fact, many men were angry that now women might be 'getting ahead', because their own lives had often left them feeling unappreciated, unsatisfied, angry and stifled.

What do men think of Women's Liberation?

'I think Women's Liberation is great. It has not affected any of my relationships!'

'A man and woman can't live and love each other as husband and wife unless the man is the head of the house and the wife considers her husband as the master over her in everything.'

'I can't respect women, because why did they let themselves be subjugated, owned and ruled?'

'I think it's important to mention the guilt I sometimes feel very acutely when I realize the privileges I enjoy as opposed to what the majority of women enjoy. I think of all the hidden ways that this privilege is handed to me by the culture in which I live, and the ways women are short-changed of those same privileges. It makes me uncomfortable to be given extra points for being a white, middle-class male with an education, but the ingredient that provides the most credence in this society is gender.'

Many of the answers to the question: 'What do you think about Women's Liberation?' brought out a huge amount of anger at women, or anger with men's own situation, their own role in society and tremendous lack of fulfilment. Many men felt that now, with the women's movement and the emphasis on women achieving more independence and equality, they were being falsely maligned and misunderstood:

'All I ever hear about these days is how brutal men are, how women are always getting fucked over by men, and how the sisterhood is gonna go it alone. Well, men get the same kind of shit, and I do not like being put in a category. I'm no better or no worse than anyone else, regardless of gender. Just like a woman, I want to be loved and give love in return.'

'There seems to be a growing stereotype of what bastards men are. Although I suppose some do live up to this stereotype, I know many men who don't (including, I believe, myself). I don't like this trend and find it similar to the black backlash against all whites once they achieved greater control over their lives…alienating even those whites who had fought alongside them for equal opportunities, etc. Some men are stronger feminists than many women. Why condemn all of us? Society has dictated not only to women the roles they should play but also to men. Men have been stereotyped and enslaved into following traditional approaches to life just as much as women, and the more moderate feminists are willing to accept this and seem to be turning towards a cooperation with men in changing society.'

Many answers seemed to imply that the Women's Movement is merely something having to do with women's 'self-esteem' rather than being a fundamental critique of the society and both men's and women's roles in it, and therefore something to which men must address themselves directly, as it involves a basic readjustment in 'their' world:

'The "movement" has not affected my relationships because the women I like do things as individuals, not as part of movements. However, if some subtle change in the general atmosphere has helped them to reach a more open state, that's good. Most, though, still want the man to take the initiative in the early stages of dating and sex. So it has not changed my relationships.'

'I feel that it has helped my wife.'

'Women's Liberation provides a medium of support for women who can't otherwise feel good about their womanhood. As such it has its benefits to our society.'

A minority of men, still misunderstanding it, said they were totally against Women's Liberation:

'It stinks. Women should be feminine, but with equal rights. American women should make men feel like men, not competitors.'

'I believe men and women are not equal. They each have their own jobs in life. Let me explain. First of all, a woman can have a child, a man cannot. He doesn't even have to be there for conception. A sperm bank can do that. A woman's skeleton matures faster than a man's. Women have faster reaction times in general. The list is endless in comparing men and women. They were each put on this earth with all their differences. However, if men and women stopped competing with each other, it would be a better world.'

'It made women feel like they can do it all, as if they don't need men to keep up a house. I think being pregnant should be the woman's natural desire.'

'I think it's the worst thing that ever happened to women and their relations with men.'

'I don't like it. The vital role women play as mothers who mould the future generation has been de-emphasized. We are on a self-destruction course. If you think we have a lot of crazies now – you ain't seen nothing. Day care centres are sadly run by people who raise children as a business. The children are second-class children, they are entitled to more. Up with Mother Power. It's all marketing and media hype. If some women want to work in this cold, often boring life outside the home, fine. But never degrade the role of the mother. Also, some women are getting socially aggressive. I'm flattered and respond – but if they didn't make advances to me I probably wouldn't go after them, therefore after the initial thrill is over I dump them, and I got a depressed liberated broad to deal with.'

'Women just need to sound off. The greatest people alive have been men, including Jesus Christ Himself. No woman has yet lived and been great enough to be the Daughter of God! Print it!'

'A farcical gyration of dykes. It has afforded me many laughs.'

The largest number of men said they were 'in favour of Women's Liberation, *but…*':

'It's OK but I wouldn't want a woman for a boss.'

'It is righting some wrongs, but also causing disruptions in established patterns which have been beneficial to society.'

'Women's Liberation is a just cause when it pursues equality of opportunity in life, and the desire to be judged as a person first, not on a prejudicial basis. But the Women's Movement is unjust when it chooses anti-male attitudes instead of the pursuit of justice. Anti-male is no better than anti-female.'

'I'm in favour of it when it comes to getting rid of discrimination, but it's overblown. Women have always been able to get what they want.'

'I am all for women being equal, but nothing they or I can do will change biological differences. It is wrong when women "want to be men", and I feel sorry for those who do. The world would be a miserable place if most men and women were not happy to be what they are. But basically I am open-minded and want to be fair, so I can't say I'm against women's liberation, but women's liberation turns me off when it becomes hatred of things masculine.'

A Time of Change For Men: Troubled Waters or Smooth Sailing?

Many men today – men of every age, not just younger men – are privately anguished over how to define their own masculinity, what it means to be a man

143

(whether or not to shave body hair is just one symptom of this malaise). The majority feel an enormous amount of pressure and frustration too, often focusing on women as the cause of it, rather than taking on the social values that need to be confronted. Many men feel that they cannot talk to other men about their frustrations with 'masculinity' – because to do so might make them look less 'masculine' to other men, as if they couldn't 'make it' as a man.

Men want to be close to women to express their emotional lives. This is especially true since, as we have seen, men learned from their fathers that closeness, personal talks and affection were not an appropriate part of a relationship with another man; men feel they can only express this part of themselves with a woman – and even then, all too many men have mixed feelings, believing that these feelings, these needs, represent weakness: needs they should not have.

Most men are cautious about falling in love. Men's first feelings on falling in love were as joyous and ecstatic as women's – in fact, this is one of the only parts of this book which could have been written by women – but after their initial feelings of happiness (and erotic attraction), most men ironically backed off or distrusted their feelings, the very feelings that had given them such pleasure. In fact, most men distrusted these feelings so much that the majority of marriages were not based on this kind of emotional intensity – at least as men in this study described their feelings about their marriages and their wives. Most men did not marry the women they had been most 'in love' with, although they emphasize that they love their wives and do not want to leave them, even when they are having regular sex with someone they care about outside the marriage.

The men in this study who most accepted traditional stereotypes of masculinity were those who were most unhappy with their lives. There has been a built-in contradiction between the so-called male lifestyle and human closeness. Lack of emotionality and closeness make men feel isolated, angry and cynical. Men today are faced with the rather formidable choice of either continuing to live their lives as in the past, feeling torn apart by constantly having to suppress and deny their own needs (and suffering with their early death rate and illnesses) – and creating something new.

Fathers and their Teenage Daughters

Fathers inspire a mixture of emotions in their teenage daughters – fear and longing, joy and fury, desire to be close and desire to be distant – contradictory emotions, as expressed by these girls:

144

'I idolized Daddy but never understood him.'

'We went places together. I never feared him. He is a lot like me. I have a hard time accepting him and I love him a lot.'

What is the reason for this confusing jumble of emotions? By the time a girl is twelve or so, according to my research, her relationship with her father often becomes quite strained, distant and alienated, sometimes entailing violent or angry outbursts. Whereas when younger, girls and their dads often had fun playing together, now there is a growing distance and frigidity. Girls feel confused and ask themselves: 'What happened? What did I do?' They often try to improve or change their behaviour, waiting for the father to 'see' that they are truly loveable 'like before'.

At this point, many fathers consciously are trying to distance themselves, having been told that playing and cuddling was all right before, but 'now that she is becoming a young woman', this must stop: 'keep your distance'. Fathers usually obey this rule, but frequently become hostile, known for their cutting criticisms and brooding silences or never being home. Part of this acceptance by men of the role assigned them, rather than a more creative development of a new kind of friendship with their daughter, goes back to the training for 'masculinity' that most boys endure in the schoolyard when they are about twelve, insisting that 'real boys don't have best friends who are girls', 'girls are only good for sex', etc. The proper stance for a real man, they learned, is to be critical and distant with women, being 'too soft on females' means a man is weak, a 'sissy'.

This new distance between the daughter and father at puberty is something girls do not always accept; they think it is (hopefully) an incomprehensible stage that will pass and wait for things to 'return to normal'. This 'waiting for a lost love to return' can become a lifelong emotional pattern, affecting future relationships with men. Living with longing and hope for approval from a distant father, a woman may later pick 'distant' men or bosses, hoping to make them 'see' her, love her. She may believe, as she did about her father, that no matter how cold or heartless, the man loves her underneath it all. This is especially true since most mothers reassure their daughters, no matter what: 'Yes, he loves you really.'

On the other hand, a number of girls feel they have a special secret closeness with their fathers, a special relationship, that they are really their father's 'favourite', despite the silences and despite the fact that such a special relationship is almost never acknowledged in words between father and daughter. Such 'unspoken alliances' can also be part of the office landscape.

Of course, fathers can have life-cycle problems to deal with that have nothing directly to do with their children. The anger many teenage girls see in their fathers correlates with feelings many men in my research describe in their forties and fifties. Many feel that although they do almost everything they should as men, taking care of the family, being there, earning a living, somehow they aren't appreciated or satisfied. Many feel empty.

Sometimes friendships between daughters and fathers flounder around the age when menstruation begins. Typically, fathers are not told when the daughter first gets her period. The girl feels that somehow it would not be 'right' to speak to him about this (either describing excitement and pride in growing up, or fear of 'smelling' or changing), while the father senses that he should be less and less close to his daughter as 'she becomes a young woman sexually'.

Potential friendships between fathers and daughters can be hampered by family politics, i.e., the position of the mother at the bottom on the family hierarchy (or at work, the position of women in the corporate hierarchy) and the girl's consequent fear of betraying the mother by befriending the father. Many girls feel they're involved in a constant balancing act. They want to 'play fair' and not offend either side. Also, when fathers treat their daughters as 'mere females', 'not important', trivializing their interests and work, daughters are pressured to try communicating via other means, i.e., subtle flirtation, etc.

Perhaps it is no wonder that many 'fathers' – in families and corporations – have a hard time figuring out how to relate to their 'daughters', since in the Western model of 'family', there is no type of relationship which men have with women that is not based on gender. The model is one which stresses sexuality as forming the basis of all relationships: sons and mothers, fathers and daughters, wives and husbands – friendship is not even hinted at, it is nowhere on the map.

As a girl grows up, sometimes fathers, without fully realizing what they are doing, respond to their daughters' new sexuality with misogynist ideas and anger:

'Don't wear that lipstick! You look like a prostitute!'

'You used to be my sweet little girl. What happened?'

146

Girls are usually stunned and hurt when such things are said to them. Most girls think this is not their 'real father' speaking and hope he will change back into his nicer self, the 'real him', stop this 'scary behaviour' soon. Unfortunately, most fathers never find a way to acknowledge positively (or even negatively) the onset of a girl's menstruation, the apparent changes in her body or build other bridges of communication.

Since this reproductive model of the family (the one often seen on Christmas cards and in department store windows) is actually less than 2,000 years old, it is obviously not simple 'human nature'

In families, not only fathers but also daughters worry about the nature of their 'love' for their fathers:

'My mother accused me of being flirtatious with my father. I was really very close with him, but that's not the same thing. I loved him, and he loved me, he understood me like no one else in that family.'

Some girls think they are 'guilty' of having sexual feelings for their fathers, when they are not. For example, a girl who receives gifts from her father – money, dresses, shoes, etc. – could naturally feel pleasure and excitement, which might cause her body, including her genitals, to flush with a heated, happy feeling. This flush could be confused with, or interpreted as, 'sexual arousal'. It can also be interpreted as general emotional arousal: happiness.

This self-consciousness about 'the meaning of it all' or 'fear of looking the wrong way' lends a sexual atmosphere even where there is none.

If a new friendship could come about between fathers and daughters, it would change the atmosphere of all relationships between women and men.

Public Friendships between Men and Women

Since most of us have little or no experience relating to someone of the opposite sex in any way other than through the body (our relationship may be one of blood, i.e., a father or mother or son or daughter, or it may be sexual, i.e., a wife or husband or lover), we continue to apply these layers of stereotypes to those of the opposite sex we meet, rather than allowing our minds and hearts to lead us in new directions.

Although we have a great opportunity today to create better long-term relationships and friendships between women and men, all too often relationships are overly sexualized. This is not to say that once in a while, two single people find a real relationship including a sexual relationship at work.

There is, however, such a diversity of relationships possible, a whole spectrum of relationships is not being perceived – one of the most important of these is simple friendship.

Yes, some women and men do have friendships, but these tend to be 'sotto voce' – carried on privately, rather than being accepted by others. For example, most men and women as friends do not go out to dinner alone with each other, although two men might easily have dinner together without creating gossip. If a man and a woman go out to dinner, especially more than once, people may begin to say: 'They're lovers.'

At offices, where non-sexual relationships are generally what is called for, there is still very little awareness of the great potential of trying to form new kinds of relationships and friendships with people of the opposite sex – long-term friendships that include spending time together. Some CEOs or company managers try to solve the 'problem' by declaring sexual relationships off-limits to employees. But of course half the people who work in any given company are single, and therefore it is natural and inevitable that they will fall in love and have affairs with other (hopefully single) people who work next to them. In these cases, it is usually the women who are punished, if discovered. In this sense, company presidents are like fathers who don't like their 'daughters' to have sex or fall in love with another man: many tend to 'cast out' those young women they have hired who are 'found to have a sexual liaison at work'. Such male executives in companies are sexualizing the situation by implying that 'lots of sex will go on without the rule'.

Similarly, some corporations have a problem with 'pregnant women working' – but this could be because they don't like visible signs of female sexual activity, not because pregnant women are less productive – i.e., because a pregnant stomach is a visible sexual reference implying that the woman 'had sex' and 'enjoyed it'.

There is still, in most of our psyches, the old archetype of a 'good woman' being someone like the Virgin Mary, the pure, asexual woman and mother and 'the bad woman' being a 'sexual temptress', an Eve who is sexually wicked and deserves to fall. In paternalistic management styles, the father is like God or Moses, and a woman or 'daughter' should be like Mary before she had Christ. If she has sex or gets pregnant, she becomes 'the bad girl' like Eve, who had to be banished from the Garden of Eden. Thus, pregnant women must be banished from all corporate gardens.

But how can things change? How can a father or a boss at work express his feelings of friendship and admiration for a woman, enjoy working with her and not be sexually misunderstood, create a new type of relationship that is seen for what it is? Probably in the beginning, many people, both men and women, will be misunderstood. Our society has few models for friendship between women and men. Unfortunately, the idea is frequently presented that a 'real man' feels sexually attracted to lasciviously 'younger females.' A 'real man' is one who must 'feel sexual around women'; a woman 'should naturally feel sexual around a man'. This may not be what a man or woman is feeling at all, but where is the vocabulary and understanding for expressing and creating any other close, long-term scenario?

In fact, there is a great need for a new kind of friendship between women and men. It can start between fathers and daughters, or later – it can start at any point in life between people of any age, related or not.

Many men today, as much as women, want to change the atmosphere and have better relationships, but it is difficult for men to behave differently since they rightly perceive that not conforming to being 'one of the guys' could cost them their job or their place in society – it is safer to relate to women in the traditional way, i.e., a 'real man' relates to women in terms of sex and childbearing.

More and more men and women today are finding the courage to become friends for life with each other, unembarrassed about not 'bringing the relationship to a sexual conclusion' and pleased to let others know about their friendship.

Chapter Seven

Is Homosexuality Natural?

Why do some people prefer gay sex? Why do they fall in love with each other romantically? Traditionally, what is called sex has been an activity that, by definition, was *ipso facto* heterosexual: sex 'obviously' had to be done between two people of the 'opposite' (opposing?) sexes in order to lead to reproduction. It was the premise of our social order that the only purpose of 'the sex drive' was because of the physiological need for reproduction; people said any other kind of sexual activity would not be 'natural'.

But sex is not as obviously linked to 'the need for reproduction', as some of might have wanted. As one example: why is the female orgasm not necessary for reproduction to occur? Another example: why are some people attracted to people of the same sex, why do they fall in love with a person of the same sex?

While some experience the 'desire to make love' as a desire for heterosexual coitus, others experience other feelings. In the 1870s, two German 'sexologists' came up with the term 'homosexual' to label and categorize same-sex activity; prior to that, this special term did not exist. 'Lesbian' is also a relatively recent designation, historically, referring to the Isle of Lesbos in ancient Greece, where Sappho the poetess, supposedly a lesbian based on her lovely poems, lived in ancient times. Alfred Kinsey brilliantly explained almost sixty years ago that he believed 'homosexual' and 'lesbian' should only be used as adjectives to describe activities, not adjectives to label people – especially since people have the capacity to change their sexual orientation during a lifetime (sometimes more than once).

Is it possible that our point of view as a society should be to go beyond expanding our 'tolerance', our ability to 'accept lesbianism and homosexuality'

151

– toward making 'sex' much more diverse, to include a much larger spectrum of choices for everyone? What is normal in sex?

Our society assumes that 'sex' is 'natural behaviour' that consists of 'foreplay', followed by 'penetration' and intercourse, best had in a context of reproduction inside a family; the further assumption is that no matter how 'sexy', sex should still 'naturally' culminate with 'the act' (of reproduction, i.e., coitus) as the full, 'natural' expression of 'the sex drive'.

Heterosexuality became the dominant form of sexuality about 3,000 years ago (despite what many think: that sex has been 'forever' the same, it has 'always been like that'). Before that, eroticism was seen and expressed quite differently; clichés referring to 'the world's oldest profession', as if women had always 'by biology' been ordained to 'provide coital services' to men as men's basic source of pleasure, are ahistorical stereotypes used to prop up the dominant sexual ideology.

Too much of our natural eroticism has been channelled by the social order into reproductive rites, rites we are urged to repeat over and over with a partner (either inside marriage, or in the context of singles who 'meet and mate'). Although traditional heterosexual sexual activity can be beautiful, why should it be the only good way in which people can relate? Or the only way 'civilization can continue'? People have lived and reproduced in various kinds of societies; think of the antique Greeks (who had a completely different conception of sexuality and eroticism and morality), or civilizations from Polynesia to Brazil to Africa and South America that existed without insisting that only one definition of sex was morally correct and good. In our view, not only is there only one way that physical sexuality should 'appropriately' be expressed, but additionally, not to do so is to be 'immoral'; only one way of having sex is 'moral', 'right' and 'good'.

Many theories and beliefs justifying the 'naturalness' of heterosexual reproductive impulses have grown up over the last 2,000 years – when there was pressure to channel all erotic feelings into a reproductive scenario, with most other activity being declared evil and morally reprehensible, including oral sex.

Is it true that lesbian women follow a more 'natural' sexual path than homosexual men, that lesbians are more 'natural' than male homosexuals? While gay women are less visible on the streets in Gay Pride marches and so on – one sees many more men together than female couples or single gay women – statistically, there are as many gay women as gay men around the world. Many of these women report that they experience their physical relationship with another woman as completely natural, although there is no pattern to sex, nor (of course) any reproductive aim. Coitus is not, obviously, the focal point; penetration is not drenched with the heavy symbolism that heterosexual penetration of a woman by a man is – although it may have emotional symbolism.

I am not trying to add my voice to 'liberal voices' saying that homosexuality and lesbianism are 'fine alternatives'. While that may be true, the idea of tolerance seems to imply condescension, to arrogantly proclaim that there is a standard 'good' way to have sex, then 'other ways' that we should tolerate as 'alternatives', because we are good people...or something like that.

In fact, various conceptions of 'sex' could all be equally good; our idea of the sexual or erotic could be expanded so that 'a thousand flowers bloom'. One of the most important changes to address in this transformation is to speak against the oppression of women in the traditional institution of 'sex', and to show how both male and female sexual identity can be conceptualized in new and better ways.

The Glorification of Intercourse – but what about Homosexuality?

Specifically, women with other women have more orgasms than most women with men. Men have a different type of sex with other men than they do with women, and orgasm in more varied ways. It is sometimes difficult for us to see these facts clearly, since we are indoctrinated with the idea that 'sex' exists for purposes of reproduction (and that that is why nature has put the 'sex drive' into men's bodies...); yet my view is that we have been living with an ideological version of 'sex' that has narrowed all sexual feeling into a reproductive scenario, one which glorifies coitus to such an extent that we now find it difficult to get in touch with our 'other' physical ways of touching the world.

Why and how did this sexual ideology begin? In addition to practical reasons for controlling sexuality (to maintain the form of social organization we know), in the early period of the changeover to patriarchy there were political reasons as well. Other forms of sexuality represented rival forms of social organization. For example, it is generally accepted by Bible scholars that the earliest Jewish tribes mentioned in the Old Testament accepted cunnilingus and homosexuality as a valid part of life and physical relations, as did the societies around them, according to Alfred Kinsey's famous report on *Sexual Behaviour in the Human Male*. In fact, prior to the seventh century BCE[1] homosexual and other sexual activities may have been associated with Jewish religious rites, just as in surrounding cultures. But as the small and struggling tribes sought to build and consolidate their strength and social order, binding all loyalty to the one male god, all forms of sexuality except the one necessary for reproduction were banned by religious code. The Holiness Code, established at the time of their return from the Babylonian exile, sought to fence out the surrounding cultures and set up rules for separating off the religious Israelis (the Chosen People of God). It was then that non-heterosexual, non-reproductive sexual acts were condemned as the way of the Canaanite, the way of the pagan. These activities were originally proscribed as an indication of allegiance to another culture, an adjunct to idolatry – and not as 'immoral' or as sexual crimes, as we consider them. They were political crimes.

These codes have generally continued in our religious and civil law up to this day. Judeo-Christian codes still specifically condemn most sexual activity that does not have reproduction as its ultimate aim. Our civil law is largely derived from these codes, and the laws of most US states condemn non-coital forms of sexuality (in and out of marriage) as punishable misdemeanours or crimes. Thus, intercourse has been institutionalised in our culture as the only permissible form of sexual activity. Forms of sexuality other than intercourse are now also considered psychologically abnormal and unhealthy.

However, Kinsey (who was originally a biologist specializing in the gall wasp) explained that the full spectrum of physical contact is enjoyed by the other mammals, and their mental health has not been questioned. Furthermore, intercourse is not the main focus of their sexual relations, but only one activity out of many. They spend more time on mutual grooming than they do on specifically sexual contact, as Jane Goodall and other primate researchers have described in detail. They also masturbate and have homosexual relations quite commonly. Among the animals for whom these activities have been recorded are rats, chinchillas, rabbits, porcupines, squirrels, ferrets, horses, cows, elephants, dogs, baboons, monkeys, chimpanzees and many others. Although our culture seems to assume that since sexual feelings are provided by nature to insure reproduction, and therefore intercourse is or should be the basic form of our sexuality – even though women's sexual

154

feelings are often strongest when women are not fertile – it is patently obvious that other forms of sexuality are just as natural and basic as intercourse.

Chapter Eight

Sex And Age: Are Older Men Happy?

Can you love more and better, more deeply, when you are older? Can you be as excited sexually? They say one falls most deeply in love when young – later loves are limp 'also-rans'. This might or might not be true for any individual. The cliché grew up because for millennia it was needed to encourage those of reproductive age to start families. The focus on youth as more sexually active probably had something to do with society trying to motivate those of reproductive age to have coital sex and therefore reproduce.

According to my research, people in their forties, fifties, sixties often fall in love but feel they are 'silly' and don't let other people know. In fact, people over forty often fall more deeply in love than people in their twenties. This does not mean people in their teens and twenties experience less strong feelings, but that they aren't able to go as far with those feelings as they could; they don't survive the emotional ups and downs long enough to fall in love as deeply as they could. Often still self-protective, defensive and lacking in self-confidence, emotional turbulence (commonly experienced in love) causes them to seek refuge in various postures ('I'm cool. Who needs you?') that confuse the other person, who adopts a similar posture, leading to a break-up. It takes time to develop the self-confidence necessary to put one's ego aside and ignore the various clichés about what love should be, when you should love or whether a man should love a woman more, or a woman should love a man more, etc.

This is not to say that 'older love' is serene, always confident (i.e., boring). Older love affairs involve the same exquisite doubts about whether the other person 'really loves me too', anger at being apart, jealousy, fear, pride – the works. The only real difference is that rarely does one see older couples walking hand in hand on the street after work, looking like a couple, not afraid to show it.

What about sex? Perhaps one can love more deeply when older, but is sex as exciting? Do older people really get passionate and sweaty? Older love affairs can be really hot. Studies done by Masters and Johnson during the 1960s, measuring strength of contractions during orgasm, found that contractions in forty-year-old men and women were as strong or stronger than those in people in their twenties. Another researcher, M. J. Sherfey, demonstrated that the interior female sexual structure is designed in such a way that older women can experience deeper orgasm than younger women. Kinsey showed that women in their forties were more likely to orgasm with regular partners than younger, newly married women. My own research shows that women in their fifties feel an enormous increase in self-confidence that can enable them to throw off self-doubts that held them back sexually in earlier years. My research also showed that a significant minority of women in their forties and fifties (often divorced women) begin sexual relationships with another woman for the first time, and in large part these are partnerships that endure.

There is no longer any doubt that women like sex after menopause – they have orgasms, fantasies, like wearing seductive clothes, kissing and flirting – but are often ridiculed for this, whereas younger women are expected to try to be 'sexy'.

Clichés about sexuality in older men are even worse. A socially created focus on erection lessens men's enjoyment of sexuality: this focus makes them prisoners to their penis. While full erection feels good to men, and this is part of the reason men want erections, men are also educated to feel shame and guilt if they do not have erections; thus the whole issue becomes the centre of nervousness as much as pleasure. Having an erection is not the *sine qua non* of male sexuality; men can enjoy sex in many ways, with or without an erection. Although physical problems can arise as a man gets older, they are far less frequent than men are led to believe. A man's erections can become less full due to lessened blood flow around the penis, but also – even more commonly – due to semi-boredom with the stages of love; they begin to seem repetitive. Sex and 'the chase' become less interesting, men say, after spending a few years in these 'sports'.

The tragedy is that men are denied a fulfilling sexual development of themselves – by a culture that channels their sexual feelings into the service of reproduction, telling them 'a drive for penetration' is what they must feel to be 'normal' – and ironically, insisting that men have the best of all possible worlds sexually. For example, recent media debates about Viagra assume a 'common understanding' that an erection is automatically every man's goal, that men go downhill sexually after the age of twenty-one (!) and that a man has 'a problem' if his penis is not stiff and erect (how often?).

Although erection brings men physical pleasure, it also brings them psychological pleasure: part of the thrill is the image – looking 'fully sexual' and 'manly' (nothing to laugh at!). But men's sexuality is multifaceted: mature men desire diverse states of arousal, a variety of sexual events, being made love to as well as making love to someone, even missing orgasm at times.

We are all, in a way, sexual retards, trying to repeat throughout life one scenario of sexuality when the whole world is open to us.

Chapter Nine

Male Psychology, Sex And World Peace

Heroic Actions and Fear: The Janus-Headed Mentality

Glorious, heroic images of masculinity abound in history: mythic figures who sail out to find their destiny, rescue their countries, create great science and art. These heroic efforts seem to imply no negative attitudes toward women – except, of course, women were not allowed on any of these expeditions. The heroic quest has been a male preserve. Although there are a few noble images of women contained in standard history books, for example, those of women ruling their countries – Catherine of Russia, Empress Maria Theresa of the Holy Roman Empire and Queen Elizabeth I of England, to mention only the best known. But generally, when not born to it, the role of hero has been reserved for men. When Jeanne d'Arc, for example, lived a heroic life on her own initiative and in male terms, she was eventually tried as a witch and killed. Parliaments and scientific expeditions today still contain only a small number of women compared to a large number of men. How does this affect men?

To be 'male' and admired by other men seems to have two traditions: masculinity as being courageous, brave and noble; and masculinity as being macho with women, aggressive and competitive with others, 'conquering nature'. Which is the 'real' masculinity?

How can such a tradition as the noble male – going into space, building mathematical systems, discovering the laws of the universe – exist side by side with the lowly tradition of oppressing women – keeping women out of educational institutions, excluding women from power in governments and generally treating women as second-class, even less than fully human? How is one to reconcile in one's mind that a great tradition could also contain the least noble of traditions?

Has there always been this split in the culture's possibilities offered to men? Or is the 'macho' side of being male more with us today? When I asked him what he thought about 'masculinity', Gore Vidal, the famous writer, quipped: 'Oh, masculinity – I hear they had a bad outbreak of it down near Tampa, but I think now they're getting it under control.'

Historically, the classical Greek state, so admired for its balanced ideas of government and philosophy, was, we remember, not balanced: it was a male, upper-class democracy – excluding women and slaves from free speech and government, already using the stereotypes of the 'talkative' woman. Socrates' wife was said to 'nag' him, while the only philosophical women or women of letters were categorized as 'mistresses'. Does this mean they had lovers? That they were not married? That famous men were attracted to them, and they allowed these men to make love with them? Men who have lovers are not categorized by history as 'lovers', and yet women are frequently presented by the history books as no more than 'mistresses', 'harlots' or 'courtesans,' such as Madame Pompadour in eighteenth-century France.

At puberty, boys are faced with pressure to prove that they are 'one of the guys' by showing disrespect or domination over their mother in public. Most boys find this very upsetting, according to my research. Although they eventually must accept this and demonstrate their status over her, lest they risk non-acceptance by other boys and men, they then ingest a system based on a double standard that can create a bisected, Janus-headed mentality – one that believes magnificent, heroic behaviour should be displayed with other men, but with different behaviour shown towards women. They learn to respect male heroic traditions while they learn to look down on 'things female'. This sets up a psychological dichotomy, plus an inner moral compromise, that many men have difficulty overcoming later in life. How can a man think of himself as 'noble and heroic' while at the same time 'keeping a woman in her place'?

Of course this psychology is not something a man automatically adopts just because he is anatomically male; it is an imposed way of life and way of thinking. Some men confront the issues discussed here; others do not.

Most men look to women for love; 90 percent get married during their late twenties. Rarely are men the ones to initiate divorce. Men want a home, warmth and children, just as women do. But they also have deeply ambiguous feelings: real closeness is a threatening state of emotionality that most men can't afford, since a 'real man' never completely lets his guard down or loses control of a situation; a man must continually assert his 'independence' (or 'dominance'). Real closeness is forbidden for a man because it makes him vulnerable.

So exactly what is heroic in men? If many men experience their minds as being in conflict over how they should behave in 'matters of the heart', how does this conflict affect their decisions? In fact, this 'two minds' situation often plays havoc with men's logic, tricking men into believing that only by 'following the tried and true path' are they being 'rational' – no matter what their experience may tell them.

The basic ideological structure of 'male psychology' is only beginning to be understood – for many centuries it was thought to emanate automatically from 'human nature', rather than being part of a social system, not the 'essential nature' of human beings – one which can be analyzed.

What is heroism in this setting?

Oedipus and War

Middle Eastern or global wars, terrorism and how boys learn to be 'tough' and 'cool' at puberty – are they connected? Endless articles are written about 'how terrible' the wars and terrorist bombings of the last few years have been – and they are – but few are written about possible ways of ending them. So let's ask: what is the cause of the current terrible killings and bombings in the Middle East? They have gone on for a long time, not only in the Middle East but also in other parts of the world, for example, between the Irish and British, between ETA and the Spanish government, between the Tamil Tigers and the Sri Lankan authorities, or the Mexican freedom fighters and the Mexican government.

Is it simply 'human nature' to fight, so that living in a world full of tragic wars is inevitable? Or is there something we can do?

I would like to suggest 'one big global solution', which is not to say that there is a simplistic panacea for today's problems, but I do believe that there is a significant avenue of change that is not being addressed. I doubt that it is necessary to have so many wars as we are having now. While of course poverty is one of the biggest causes of feelings of resentment, there are other issues involved, specifically those that push a value system on men and boys that says 'a real man must be on top', whether in relation to the family a corporation, a society or a government.

How could we change the climate from one of war and aggression to one of negotiation, looking for more areas of agreement? One of the causes for the kinds of atrocious 'modern wars' we are seeing today is the increasing bullying of boys at puberty, the increasing glorification of 'being tough'.

Lest anyone imagine that raising children differently means change will take a long time and that we will have to wait over twenty years for the next generation to show any improvement, I would like to point out an immediate application that could make a difference within days or weeks. If we agree that bullying of boys to 'be tough' and to look down on those who are 'weak' leads to a way of fighting that is not productive, then why not immediately ban all forms of bullying?

Getting to the bottom of the tough-guy mentality has been part of my research. What I discovered is that the bullying of boys at school plays the biggest part in making 'men' conform to, or fear showing disrespect for, the system of values of 'the tough guys' – whether at work, in the office or on the playground. We can change this. If we would ban the bullying of boys, make it an offence – for example, bigger boys bullying younger or smaller boys should be punished, shown not to be succeeding (at present they are) – we could change the mentality of the culture. Oedipus needs to grow up in a new way.

Sex and Peace: Make Love not War

How is sex political? This is often heard, but what does it really mean?

Unravelling the hidden rules behind what we are told is 'the right way to have sex and pleasure' is key to understanding the construction of the entire social system; therefore understanding the ideology underlying sex will go a long way toward enabling individuals and society to become more egalitarian and less warlike, more peaceful. A new sexuality is part of an emerging new politics of planetary health, the environment, issues of 'globalization' or 'anti-globalization' and world peace.

This vision of sex is connected to a new international value system that is trying to emerge – a still hazy, revised view of who we are as a species on the planet, what we are doing or should be doing with our lives. The central question of this new value system remains one of war and peace: why are there so many wars, is war an inevitable consequence of human nature? Could we be less warlike?

In its deepest sense, sexuality is connected to world peace, and not because of a superficial notion that 'sex' is 'deep'. Since sexuality is a key element in women's growing 'equality' and activity in the world, central to the definition of 'who a woman is', and because sex is key to 'who a man is', if a man rethinks his primary assumptions about sex, he will also revamp his ideas about himself and who he is as a man, society will be greatly affected.

No one should think that saying 'sex is connected to world peace' means that 'if people have more and better sex, they will be more satisfied, and therefore they will be less interested in war'. While undoubtedly true, and while the slogan 'Sex, Peace and Love' is good, the idea proposed here is something new: that through the physical movements of 'the sex act', individuals learn lessons in gender behaviour and 'proper psychology' that shape thinking and belief systems – that gender as taught to children is largely inculcated through sexual values and moral codes as we know them; thus if we critique what sex is, as we are doing here, we can begin to see ourselves (and human life) as separate from this ideology, and therefore innovate a more positive future.

The radical new analysis of male sexuality I am presenting in *Oedipus Revisited* shows how the construction of boys' sexual identity at puberty and even earlier carries over into men's identity as adults: if boys are brought up to think that being a man means being sexually 'big' and financially powerful, and the idea is pushed that a 'real' man must be 'cool and tough' – although 'sensitive' – then anyone who does not 'show proper respect' should be 'taught a lesson' and 'the right reaction' for an adult man is an aggressive posture, not dialogue. The current belief in 'sex drive' as an inevitable hormonal mechanism inside men props up this system, asserting that men are 'by nature' aggressive and need to be dominant, that 'dominance' and 'command' are inherent to men's 'psychology'. In my thesis, the social commands to boys (a sort of software programming in the brain) are causing an exaggeratedly militaristic society; these software commands are unjustified and can be changed, once they are identified, thus ending a major cause of today's wars, small and large. Wars are fought when dialogue is discontinued... Beginning to deconstruct 'male sexuality' is thus doing two things: creating more pleasure and space for individual men and helping society develop a more peaceful global strategy.

Most people today are concerned about how they should feel about sex in their private lives; they are also concerned by heated debates about sex in the news, i.e., public discussions of abortion, parity and equality, sexual harassment, the *chador* as 'necessary' for a woman to wear to express 'modesty' and 'humility', as opposed to the 'secular' miniskirt, the sexual trafficking in women and rape in war. Most people fear they have fantasies that are not 'politically correct', and often cannot reconcile their personal sexual desires with what they believe to be ethical. This discussion should help anyone trying to sort out these thoughts.

In the end, sex and social reality are connected. As noted, the analysis begins here with a sharp focus on the clitoris and female orgasm then expands in ever-widening circles to various related matters until we encompass the entire society, because sexuality is so deeply connected to society. The definition of both female and male sexuality is central to our culture's social structure. If you believe that the female orgasm happens for most women with some form of clitoral stimulation, then this brings into question many of our most sacred beliefs about 'the act', who men are by their nature and who women are.

No one should fear the changes; sex can be much better and 'sexier' than it is. Revising this institution does not mean making it 'politically restricted', no longer 'sexy' or 'fun'. In fact, we should be able to display more of our sexual fantasies, even if 'incorrect', become more 'who we are' after this revision than before.

Redesigning Sexuality

How to devise a 'new sexuality'? I propose we go back in time to discover the original meaning of our sexual feelings and desires as children... How can an individual know the original meaning of sexuality? When you were a child, what were your first sexual thoughts? How did you feel about your sexuality the first time you had an orgasm? Try to remember... Could we today rediscover our original feelings and deprogram our brains so that we would be able to construct a new sexuality based on what those forgotten feelings tell us?

There is merit in addressing sex itself in order to deconstruct it. Sex has been a grossly sexist institution oppressive to women and to men. Today it can become a personal expression of a wide-ranging sensual-sexual vocabulary that individuals want to use – not overlooking either women's or men's rights.

Reinventing sexuality means going back to basics: what do women want? What do men want? Is it the clichés of 'male desire' we see in porno magazines? Who would want sex without the overall head-to-toe physical

166

contact it involves? This is one example of parts of erotic contact becoming undervalued by the lack of vocabulary.

Although some would think that 'if only men would understand the female orgasm, sex would be fine', there is much more involved in today's changes than that – worthy as that may be. First, many women today are making sexual exchanges take a profoundly new direction, not by being 'dominatrices' but by focusing on discovering what pleases them and involving men in these activities, rather than giving over autonomy, playing the part expected, being enslaved by the ideology with its 'old dance steps', the choice being either 'passivity' or 'dominance'.

The social system as we have known it fetishizes 'gender' – whether you are female or male – making these the two most basic categories of existence: aren't you asked on every banking and insurance form to state if you are male or female? Although feminists in the US during the 1970s fought to make this illegal, arguing that it usually worked against women by discriminating against them due to stereotypes in the minds of reviewers, these questions are still routinely asked on most institutional applications. Yet it is possible to envision a society in which gender is not the basic focus, nor are the 'two sexes' trained to go in different directions with their needs and desires, how they see the world.

The way sex has been and is being defined makes men – who are more laden with power, thus 'guilty' and 'arrogant' *vis-à-vis* women and psychologically alienated from themselves – and women simultaneously long for and fear each other. Just think how many men fear 'performance pressures'. This is easily seen, for example, in the popularity of drugs like Viagra that show men still believe in the talisman of a 'hard penis' as their ticket to intimacy and 'good performance'. How many women fear that they do not have orgasm 'the right way', that they cannot orgasm during 'the act' or are not pretty enough or thin enough? These worries need not exist, were it not for a definition of sex that sets men and women against each other. A simple acceptance of the scientific fact of the wonderfully easy and pleasurable way that women have orgasm can set both men and women free from these performance worries – and their fear of the other. Of course this change should be accompanied by a simultaneous economic improvement, so that men and women are no longer economic enemies; at present, women in the West earn approximately 30 percent less than men in similar employment, while women worldwide are the world's poorest group.

There is no real opposition between a human being who is male and a human being who is female. The social system, denying female human beings their rights in terms of voting and even owning property or having their own money – and the religious system, for centuries declaring women had no souls, murdering women by burning them at the stake, justifying this by a desire to 'purify' society – have set men and women against each other. Most men have bought into this system, believing that they were being given better status and more rights and privileges.

If society creates 'human nature', as proposed in my theories (and those of Jean-Jacques. Rousseau, Thomas Paine and others), then the positive news here is that we can change it by our actions. If we analyze 'sexual nature', we are investigating the major underpinning of what is called 'human nature' and its meaning. The body, important and wonderful as it is, is only part of who we are sexually; much of how we decide to use our bodies in sexuality comes directly from the culture – a culture that we create every day. Some say 'human nature' is fixed, unchangeable, but this is not true; human history and culture go back something like 20,000 years; our version of 'human nature' is only approximately 2,000 or 3,000 years old, if that.

This work aims to help in transforming the age-old face-off in the heart of the relationship between the genders, otherwise known as sexual relations, and thus make a more harmonious and satisfying way of life for everyone.

Sex and Globalization

Sex and human rights are connected. The globalization of values such as 'human rights' means that whatever values of sex are disseminated (via pornography, mass media and popular culture) tend to be the values of the new international global system – like it or not, say it's good or bad.

Therefore we should re-evaluate sex, not only for ourselves, but in order to build a positive and lasting partnership with other cultures who receive their view of the West as much from pornography and pop media versions of sex (and all the values attached), as from the Western corporate presences, market mechanisms and government policies.

I believe there is a totally new way of seeing eroticism and sex that includes equality and is also 'sexier' than the current idea of the sex act. Changing what have been extremely damaging versions of sex will form an important fundamental basis for a new psychology that is more peaceful, less warlike.

Our idea of sex is now being spread around the world, the trendy underside of globalization: for example, T-shirts worn under suits sport English words such as 'sex', while a hip chain of clothing uses the name FCUK, an obvious play on the Anglo-Saxon word 'fuck'.

Western sexual display is as much part of 'globalization' as designer labels or Coca-Cola. This idea of sex is being diffused throughout the world via pornography, the Internet, magazines and films. It looks 'hip and new', but is basically archaic and sexist: a way of congratulating oneself on being 'modern and young' while being safely out of date. When will sexual clichés catch up with who 'the new woman' and 'new man' are?

These slogans, omnipresent in media around the world, seem to be the partners of 'the new global democracy' and 'all that is new', so that many younger people all over the world somehow wish to adopt these fashions and products, even at the same time that they may protest Western policies of war and 'economic imperialism'. These 'symbols of the West' carried in advertising and in Internet pornography are highly visible and seductive for many. Sex seems to have nothing to do with 'politics of war and peace' on the surface.

What are our values going to be in this new international, multicultural world? Unquestionably, the values of the West are playing a big part in shaping global ideals. Although much lip service is paid to 'respecting that the cultures of other societies are different' and 'have as much right to their views as we do', in fact, the status of Western ideas has an undeniable glamour for many.

In this context, pornographic sexual values – whether in films, advertising or on the Internet – represent themselves as 'new' and 'part of the modern West'. In fact, pornography is the major vehicle spreading the values and definitions of 'the new sexuality' (Western trendiness). Ironically, just when sexual values are changing in the West, the outdated sexual values of the past are becoming the 'new thing' in other cultures, robbing them of their own version of sexual expressions of body and spirit ('not modern enough'). Many cultures show more diversity of sexual expression than our own, that is, the languages contain a more diverse vocabulary; for example, our term 'sex' has no equivalent in other languages, so that around the world the English word 'sex' is being adopted (especially by those 'young and hip'), as well as the word 'fuck'. This changes the focus of what goes on between people in private, especially as men are designated the 'fuckers' (active makers of sex), and women the 'fuckees' (those who receive sex: 'good girls don't do it'). Female 'equality' is not countenanced in many 'developing' countries.

Ironically, the values of 'human rights' and 'justice' are becoming strong around the world, often in the very same groups that embrace Western versions of 'sex'. How to account for this irrational combination? Similarly, in the West there is a vast gap separating most people's idea of sex and the ideals of human rights and global peace. One is not thought to be connected to the other. Or one can hear it said: 'Yes, of course, there is the issue of women's rights, but this is an extremist idea that need not be addressed just at the moment when momentous matters of war and peace are at hand…' Human rights activists do not generally speak about 'the details of sex', except in terms of an issue such as trafficking of women or rape in war. It is even said that pornography showing woman as a 'dominatrix' is the proof that today's pornography is 'modern' and 'gives women equal rights'!

In some parts of the world, a revulsion against these images of sex is creating a religious revival as people of all ages look for another way of life that does not include these images with their values and way of life.

In fact, the values of human rights and world peace are much nearer to those of sex (as we need to redefine it; this does not mean showing women as either submissive or dominatrix) than is usually imagined. Human rights for men, in connection with sex, have to do with an end to the macho brainwashing that leads them to believe that during sex, they become brainless animals who want to 'fuck their eyeballs out' with no thinking, that they were 'born to dominate women that way'.

Both women's and men's rights are being violated by current ideas considered 'trendy', in fact, the male psyche is being continuously constructed and reconstructed via propaganda about male sexuality, through jokes about male virility and clichés about 'who men are by nature', etc. A new way of defining the nitty-gritty of sex and intimate exchanges can serve as a solid basis in daily life for a new system of global ethical values.

This book charts a course that is neither 'a return to family values' with its compromised double standard of sexual morality, nor a spastic leap into 'the new hip world of sexual experimentation and shock' (woman as dominatrix – man as raging beast) but sets out a third way to go forward in private life, describing a landscape rich in eroticism and dignity.

Appendix

Research Questionnaire on Men and Male Sexuality[1]

Readers are requested to send their answers to these questions, or whichever questions they wish, to hite2000@hotmail.com or by post to Professor Shere Hite c/o
Arcadia Books, 15-16 Nassau Street, London W1W 7AB, UK.

The purpose of this questionnaire is to better understand how men feel about their lives. Since so many of our society's ideas about who men are and who men should be -- perhaps made most explicit in "sex" -- are stereotyped, it is hard to know what men as individual human beings really feel. It means a great deal that you answer, and thus perhaps contribute to developing a more positive and caring way of life, and a better understanding of sex. The results will be published as an extended discussion of the replies, including many quotes, in the same format as The Hite Report on Female Sexuality. The replies are anonymous, so don't sign your answers. It is not necessary to answer every single question – answer only those which interest you, but please answer!

I.   Your Early Sexual Memories
1.   What are the earliest sexual feelings you can remember, for example, touching yourself during a bath? How old were you?
2.   When did you first masturbate? To orgasm? How old were you?   Did you learn by yourself, from someone else, or from films?

[1]   Research for the earlier Hite Report on Male Sexuality was conducted between 1974 and 1981 when a version of this questionnaire for men, slightly changed here, was used.

3.   At what age did you reach your first full orgasm? Ejaculate? Did you orgasm before you were old enough to ejaculate? Did you get intense pleasurable feelings from touching yourself before puberty?   Did you have wet dreams during sleep?

4.   Were you told about sex by your parents? What did they tell you? What did your friends tell you?

5.   When did you first hear about menstruation, and what did you hear?

6.   Did your sexual feelings change as you grew up? What were your ideas about sex – during childhood, grade school and later high school?

7.   How has your sex life changed over the years? Does age affect sex? Has your enjoyment of sex changed?

8.   Have you ever tried drugs like 'Viagra' or 'Ciallis' to enhance erection? What was your experience like?

9.   Do activities like sunbathing, lounging in a bathrobe on the couch (watching tv? with a sex partner?), sleeping with someone, or playing with children or pets, play a part in your overall bodily satisfaction -- in addition to sex? Which do you like?

10.   How often do you usually have "sex" -- with a partner or with yourself (masturbation)?

11.   Does hanging out with friends play a part in your overall feeling of well-being? How important is it?

12.   How important is home and/or family life, and what parts do you enjoy?

13.   Do you like touching and holding children?   Snuggling with them? Wrestling? Giving them baths? Rocking them? Feeding them?

14.   Have you ever wished you could be a mother? How did you feel when you found out men couldn't bear children? (glad? sorry?)

15.   What do you think of the role of being a father (whether or not you are a father)?

16.   Do you enjoy physically caring for a child or a needy adult? How do you do it? Were you prepared to do this by your parents?

17.   Where have you found the most warmth and closeness in your life?

18.   Would you like more time to yourself?

19.   How do you feel about privacy in the bathroom? Do you close the door? Do you sometimes like for your partner to be in the bathroom with you during urination or defecation? Do you like to see your partner urinating, etc.? Taking a bath or shaving?

II.   Your Masculinity

20.   What is your age and background – occupation, education, upbringing, religion, race, and anything else you consider important?

21.   What do you look like? Do you consider yourself handsome, pretty plain, ugly – or no comment?

22.   How would you define masculinity? Are you masculine? How masculine are you?

23.   What is the difference between masculine and "macho"? How would you rate yourself on the "macho" scale from one to ten?

24.   What qualities make a man a man? That is, what qualities do you admire in men? Are you proud of your masculinity?

25.   What did your father tell you about how to be a man? What did he tell you about women?

26.   How can a man distinguish himself today? What is heroic in our time?

27.   What can men as a group be proud of? Ashamed of?

28.   What is your biggest worry or problem in your life?

29.   Is success important? Are you successful?   In what way?

30.   Do you believe in being ruthless when you have to?

31.   Do you sometimes feel hurt or sad but don't show it? Do you act angry instead? Do you force yourself to behave like a robot? Do you feel like a robot?

32.   How would you feel if you were described as having something about you that was "like a woman"?

33.   Were you ever called a "sissy"? Told "Be a man!"? What was the occasion? How did you feel?

34.   Do you envy women's freedom to be gentle and emotional, or to have a temper? Do you envy women the lack of pressure on them to make money or be hard and successful?

35.   How have women hurt you?

36.   Are there ways in which you feel guilty about how you have behaved toward a woman? How?

37.   Do you look at pornography? What kind? Did your father read pornography when you were growing up? Where/when did you first see it? Do you think you are like the men in it?

38.   Does pornography represent certain elemental truths about how men and women really are – both psychologically and sexually?

39.   Are you in agreement with the "sexual revolution"?

40.   What do you think of women's liberation? How has it affected your relationships?

41.   What do males need from females? What do you get from women that you don't get from men?

42.   Do you have more male or female friends? Why?

III.   Your Sexual Relationships

43.   Do you prefer sex with women, men, or either – or with yourself, or not at all?

44.   Do you think sex is important, or overrated?   What other things in life are more important?

45. Does sex have a spiritual significance for you?

46. Answer one of the following:

A. If you are married, how many years have you been married? Do you like being married? Why did you get married originally? What is the effect on sex? Do you love your wife? In what sense? Does she orgasm with you? From what stimulation? If you masturbate, does she know?

Do you believe in monogamy? Have you had/do you have "extramarital" sexual experiences? If so, how many? Are you having one now? What was/is the effect on you as an individual and on your marriage? Does your partner know about them? If you have children, why did you decide to have them? Did you want to be a father? How did you feel when your wife first told you you were having a baby? Do you like having children? Do you feel you had to give up some things in order to be married and/or have children? What? How would your life have been different?

B. If you are divorced, what are the reasons? How do you feel about it?

C. If you are homosexual, please answer any of the previous questions that apply to you and also: How long have you had physical and emotional relationships with men? How do they compare with relationships with women, if you have had any? Do you want to, or do you, live permanently with one man?

D. If you are "single," do you enjoy being single? What are the advantages and disadvantages? Do you plan to marry eventually? What is your sex life like?

E. If you live at home with a parent or family, what rules are set up concerning your sexual and dating activities? Have your parents discussed sex realistically with you? Sex education at school, what is/was it like? Where have you gotten most of your sexual information? From friends? Teachers? Books? Sex magazines? Family? Have you had difficulty getting accurate information on sex? If you have had a sexual relationship, do your parents know? How did they react?

If you have not yet had sex with a partner, what do you imagine it will be like?

F. If you are living with someone, please answer any of the questions above which apply. How long have you been living with them? Would you like to be married? What are your plans for the future?

G. If you are currently uninterested in sex (except for masturbation?), how long do you plan to remain "celibate"? How long have you felt this way? Is it ok to be celibate?

47. If none of these categories describe your life, please describe yourself in your own way.

Love

48. Describe the time you fell the most deeply in love. How did it feel? What happened?

49. Did you ever cry yourself to sleep because of problems with someone you loved? Contemplate suicide? Why?

50. What was the happiest you ever were with someone? The closest? When were you the loneliest?

51. How do your friendships compare with your love relationships? Which would you pick if you had to choose?

52. Do you feel you can truly love someone?

53. Is your greatest love yet to come? What are your deepest longings for a love relationship with another person?

IV. Orgasm

54. How important are orgasms to you? Can you enjoy sex without orgasm? Can you enjoy sex if your partner does not have an orgasm?

55. Please describe what an orgasm feels like -- do you feel most of the sensation in the shaft of the penis or inside the body at the base? Which feels best? How does the very best moment feel?

56. How often do you have sex without orgasm? Do you ever feel pressured to have orgasms? When?

57. How does your body react when you are having an orgasm? Tighten up? Move a lot? Stop moving? Go out of control? What facial expression do you make?

58. Do you sometimes ejaculate without experiencing orgasm? How often? Did you orgasm as a boy before you started ejaculating?

59. Have you ever continued on to a second orgasm without losing your erection? Did you ejaculate both times?

60. Is erection necessary for your sexual arousal, or can you feel aroused without erection? How are the feelings different? Does it bother you not to have an erection? What is/was your partner's reaction? Is erection more for you, or 'for her'?

61. Do you sometimes continue sex with a soft penis if you don't have an erection?

62. Are you always aroused when you have an erection, or are there other causes of erection?

63. Do you like feeling aroused for extended periods of time, or do you prefer to go on to orgasm relatively quickly? During masturbation? During sex with a partner?

V. Masturbation

64. How often do you masturbate? Do you feel pleased? ashamed? satisfied? Are you secretive or open about it?

65. Do you enjoy masturbation? Physically? Emotionally? What do you find most satisfying about it?

66.   How do you masturbate? Please describe. For example, do you hold your penis with your hand and move your hand on your penis, or do you move your whole body, rubbing against something? Is stimulation important at the top or bottom of your penis? Do you mind the wetness of ejaculation? What do you do with the ejaculated liquid? Is there any specific position you like to be in? Are there specific thoughts or fantasies you use?

67.   Can you delay your orgasm during masturbation? Which ways do you use?

68.   Do you ever stop short of orgasm when you masturbate to heighten your sexual feelings? Do you sometimes masturbate before sex (but not to orgasm) to arouse yourself?

69.   What is the importance of masturbation in your life?

VI.   Your Body -- How do you feel about it?

70.   Do you like the way your penis and scrotum look and smell? Do you like the size and shape of your genitals?

71.   Are you circumcised? Do you like this, or wish you weren't? Did you, or would you, have your son circumcised?

72.   What were your feelings when you found out about your own circumcision? Were you shocked? Pleased? Do you have a physical reaction in your genitals when you think about it?

73.   Do you remember anything about the procedure? How old were you?

74.   Has circumcision affected your attitude about your penis? How? Does having or not having a foreskin affect your sexual activities?

75.   Why are men circumcised?

76.   Does your partner like your genitals? Has a partner ever commented negatively about your genitals? How did you feel about it?

77.   Do you like fellatio -- oral stimulation of your penis? Can you usually orgasm this way? How do you like it to be done? Do you expect to have orgasm inside your partner's mouth? That your partner will swallow the semen?

78.   Do you like mouth-anal contact?

79.   Do you like manual stimulation of your penis by your partner? Do you often orgasm this way? What other parts do you like your partner to touch?

80.   Do you enjoy masturbating with another person present? Do you like having your partner masturbate him/herself when with you?

81.   Do you like (or would you like) to be rectally penetrated? By a finger? By a penis? How does it feel? Do you orgasm this way? Exactly what does anal intercourse feel like, physically and emotionally?

82.   Do you like "foreplay"? What kind of "foreplay" is important to you? How do you like to be touched, and where? Kissed? Petted? Are your breasts sensitive? Your buttocks? Your testicles? Your mouth? Your ears?

176

83. Do you get enough foreplay from your partner? Does your partner touch and fondle you enough?

84. Do you sometimes like making out without having "real sex"? Do you prefer it?

85. Who usually makes the initial sexual advance -- you or the other person?

86. Have you ever approached someone about sex and been refused? How did you feel? Have you refused someone else? Why?

87. Are there certain times when you're not interested in sex? Do you experience periodic highs and lows in your sexual interest?

VII. Friendships with Other Men and Sexual Relationships

88. Describe your best male friend. What do you like about spending time with him?

89. Do you belong to, or socialize with, a group of men? What do you like about them? What do you talk about?

90. What do you value about men's friendships? What do men mean in your life?

91. Were you in the army or military so that you lived with many other men? Did you like the camaraderie with them? Did you have any special friendships or sexual experiences with men during this time?

92. Do you enjoy participating in sports with other men? Do you like closeness with men in these activities?

93. Did you have a best friend in high school or college?

94. Are you or were you close to your father? What was/is he like?

95. Describe the man you are or were closest to in your life. In what ways are/were you dose? Do/did you spend time together? Why did/do you like him?

96. If you have not had a physical or sexual relationship with another man, would you enjoy one?

Sex with Men

97. How old were you when you had your first sexual experience with a man or boy?

98. What was the first time you ever had physical contact with a man, including cuddling or kissing, for example with your father or a relative?

99. Did you have intimate physical contact that you did not consider 'sexual'?

100. What are your favourite things about sex with men? Why would you recommend homosexuality to other men?

101. Do you like anal intercourse? Exactly what does it feel like—both physically and emotionally? Do you orgasm this way?

102. Do you like giving a man fellatio? Do you swallow the seminal fluid? Do you like it?

103. Can you orgasm from just lying down together and kissing and rubbing crotches together?

104. Are you in love? In a steady relationship? How many men in your life have you had a sexual relationship with?

105. Do you like monogamy? Do you prefer emotional closeness or casual sex or both?

106. Would you ever fall in love with a woman (again)? Why or why not?

107. Do people at work know you are gay? Do your parents?

108. Do you take an open stand on gay issues? Or do you prefer being gay in a straight world, belonging to a secret, elite society?

VIII. Feelings about Women and Sexual Relationships

109. Do you have close women friends? A sister you are close to?

110. Are you or were you close to your mother? In what way? What was/is she like? What did/do you think of her?

111. What things about women in general do you admire? Dislike? What do women contribute to society?

112. What do you think about women's liberation?

113. Are you currently in a relationship with a woman? What is she like? Why do you like her?

Sex with Women

114. Has any woman discussed her sexual feelings seriously and openly with you?

115. When did you first learn about the clitoris? Did you hear about it from other men? From women? From books?

116. Do you like giving clitoral stimulation to orgasm? How do you do it? Do you feel comfortable giving clitoral stimulation?

117. Please describe how you stimulate the clitoris with your hand, finger or tongue and lips. Do you do this until orgasm?

118. Does your partner masturbate to orgasm? How does she do it?

119. When did you first realize most women don't orgasm from intercourse? What was your reaction?

120. Do you enjoy cunnilingus with a woman? What do you most like about it? Does it depend on your feelings for your partner?

121. Do you get sexually excited stimulating your partner? Do you enjoy her orgasm? In what way? What parts of touching, feeling and kissing your partner do you enjoy most? Least?

122. How do you give the woman an orgasm? Do you prefer the woman to orgasm from coitus?

IX. What does intercourse mean to you?

123. Do you like intercourse (penis/vagina)? Do you enjoy it emotionally as well as physically? In what way?

124. What position is most enjoyable?

125. Why do you like intercourse?

126. Do you ever experience physical discomfort? Boredom? When?

127. Do you assume that every time you have sex, it will induce intercourse?

128. Would you be willing to replace intercourse with other activities during sex? Or do you prefer to define sex as intercourse?

129. Does your partner usually orgasm during sex with you? What are the signs? Do you sometimes worry she might fake orgasm?

130. Can you always tell if your partner has an orgasm? How can you tell? If in doubt, do you ask? If you ask and she says "yes," do you believe her?

131. Would you prefer to have sex with a woman who has orgasm from intercourse (coitus) rather than from clitoral stimulation?
When does the woman/women you have sex with usually orgasm? Do most women have orgasm during intercourse?

132. How do you feel if a woman stimulates herself to orgasm by using her own hand with you? During intercourse? How do you feel if she uses a vibrator?

133. Do you feel there is something wrong with your "performance," technique, or sensitivity if the woman does not orgasm from intercourse itself? That you're "not man enough," or did not do it right? That you should be more sensitive? Last longer?

134. Does it matter to you if a woman reaches orgasm during sex with you? Do you try to find out what stimulation an individual woman needs to have an orgasm?

135. Who usually reaches orgasms first, you or the woman? During which activity?

136. Has a woman ever expressed anxiety or been apologetic to you about how long she takes to orgasm, or become ready for intercourse?

137. How do you feel if your partner does not have an orgasm at all, in any way? Do you just know, or does she tell you?

138. Can you control when you come to a climax? How long can you hold off without losing your erection?

139. Does it disturb you to lose your erection? Do you stop physical activities if you don't have an erection/have intercourse?

140. Do you ever ejaculate or orgasm "too soon" during intercourse? How long do you have intercourse in these cases? Is the ejaculation/orgasm satisfying to you? Why does the situation bother you?

141. Do you use any particular method to have intercourse longer without orgasming? Does prolonged thrusting dull the sensitivity or feeling of your penis?

142. When should a man ejaculate -- should the woman be consulted? Who decides when sex is over?

143. Do you control when you come and how you have an orgasm?

144. Do you control which activities sex consists of?

145. Do you talk to other men about sex? What do you talk about? Do you brag? Do you share practical information (how-to)? Feelings of pressure or insecurity (how to do it)?

146. Why have many women traditionally not wanted sex as much as men? What kind of sex do women want most?

X. Birth Control Methods and Condoms vs. HIV/Aids

147. What contraceptive methods (birth control) do you use? Who decides? Which kind do you prefer? Are you aware of the possible side effects of the birth control pill?

148. Do you use a condom to prevent Aids/HIV or for birth control?

149. Is it difficult to put on a condom? How often do you use one? Have you ever used a condom to delay orgasm?

150. If you have a sexual relationship with a woman, do you you feel responsible for discussing birth control before intercourse? Who is responsible if she becomes pregnant? Do you ask a woman if she has taken measures to prevent conception before intercourse?

151. Does the possibility of pregnancy cause problems in your sexual relationship/s?

152. Have you ever been a party to an unwanted pregnancy? What did you do about it?

153. Are you in favour of abortion? Have you ever impregnated a woman who subsequently had an abortion? Have you been involved in helping a woman secure an abortion? Did you go with her? What was the outcome, and how do you both feel now?

154. If you have a vasectomy, how does having a vasectomy affect your sexual activities? What do your partners think about it? Have you ever wished to have it reversed? Would you recommend it to other men?

155. Do you know what vasectomy involves? Would you wish to get one? Under what circumstances?

156. Have you ever witnessed childbirth?

XI. Violence during Sex

157. Has violence been part of a sexual relationship you had? What kind? How did you feel about it?

158. Have you been excited by a physical struggle or fight – with a man or woman? Please describe.

159. Have you ever struck or hurt your lover? Why? What effect did it have? Did you feel good when you did it?

160. Are you interested in bondage? Spanking? How does it feel?

161. Is it exciting to force someone to your will, sexually -- for example, rape them?

162.   Do you find humiliation sexually arousing?

163.   Would you/have you had a sexual relationship with a very young person? How did you feel about it?

164.   How do you define rape? Is it disturbing to you? How/How not? Where do you draw the line between consent and rape?

165.   Have you ever raped a woman? If not, have you ever wanted to rape a woman? Why?

166.   Have you ever pressured a woman to have sex with you, when she didn't seem to want to? How did you do it? Did you have a line? Did it succeed? Did you enjoy sex? Are you good at it?

167.   How do you develop a sexual relationship in the direction you desire? Is it easy to remain in charge of the situation?

168.   If there is a power relationship involved in sex, who has the most power – you or your partner?

169.   Is sex political?

THANK YOU FOR ANSWERING THIS QUESTIONNAIRE!

A.   Why did you answer this questionnaire?

B.   Did you read *The Hite Report on Female Sexuality*?

C.   Do you think other men will be as honest as you were in answering this questionnaire? How honest were you?

D.   Please add anything you would like to say that was not mentioned.